SHEEP

—AMID—

WOLVES

Biblical Guide For Building Worldly Wealth
—— and ——
BECOMING FINANCIALLY FREE

RICH GOMEZ

AUTHOR
ACADEMY elite

Printed in the United States of America

Published by Author Academy Elite
PO Box 43, Powell, OH 43065
www.AuthorAcademyElite.com

Identifiers:
LCCN: 2020911879
ISBN: 978-1-64746-340-3 (paperback)
ISBN: 978-1-64746-341-0 (hardback)
ISBN: 978-1-64746-342-7 (ebook)

Available in paperback, hardback, e-book, and audiobook

All Scripture quotations, unless otherwise indicated, are taken from the Holy Bible, New International Version®, NIV®. Copyright © 1973, 1978, 1984 by Biblica, Inc.™ Used by permission of Zondervan. All rights reserved worldwide.

Any Internet addresses (websites, blogs, etc.) and telephone numbers printed in this book are offered as a resource. They are not intended in any way to be or imply an endorsement by Author Academy Elite, nor does Author Academy Elite vouch for the content of these sites and numbers for the life of this book.

Some names and identifying details have been changed to protect the privacy of individuals.

www.sheepamidwolves.com
For large orders, please email: orders@sheepamidwolves.com

TABLE OF CONTENTS

Section Three: What Is Money?

Section Four: Being a Good Steward

PREFACE

So if the Son sets you free, you will be free indeed.
—John 8:36

To begin, I want to clearly say that this book isn't meant to be a prosperity gospel. I'm also not saying that God wants us to be *rich* and live a life of luxury. But I'm saying He wants us to be good stewards of everything He entrusts us with and be blessed so we can be a blessing to others. The only way to do that is by being financially free. Freedom is what Christ wants for us all. In Galatians 5:1 we read, "It is for freedom that Christ has set us free. Stand firm, then, and do not let yourselves be burdened again by a yoke of slavery."

I don't want anyone to say we need to live a poor life, and we shouldn't want money. We are here to represent and follow in the footsteps of Jesus, and of all the great things He did, the one which stands out the most is He provided. And just like Jesus, we need to provide for our families, but living paycheck to paycheck isn't how we do it. We are to leave an inheritance as told to us in Proverbs 13:22: "A good person leaves an inheritance for their children's children." Going into debt isn't how it's going to happen.

If you're at all curious to precisely what this book is about, I can sum it up like this: It's as if Dave Ramsey and Robert Kiyosaki had a baby. It will teach things we weren't taught in school and explain how the wealthy use their money so we can do the same.

One thing to keep in mind is the need to have an inward change before we can change outwardly. This book will guide us in doing just that. Once you've read and learned the contents of this book, you'll need to apply what you've learned. That is the only way to go from an inward change to an outward change. After certain chapters, you will have steps to take. Taking these steps right after each chapter will position you with a greater chance of success. Remember, knowledge without action is useless.

> The answer to prayer is not according to your
> faith while you are talking, but according to
> your faith while you are working.
> —Wallace D. Wattles

How can we give ourselves to God if we are under stress?

This book has four purposes, with a section dedicated to each. It is okay to read it from start to finish, but you can also learn about each part and start reading from the part that is congruent with your current financial situation.

To give you more of an understanding of the book's contents, here is a breakdown of each section.

Section One: Breaking the Bad Mindset

In this section, I'll give a bit of my history about how I grew up with the *not having enough* mentality, which was a constant threat. I'll share negative concepts about the rich, living on the poverty line, and what the church says about money. These consistent false doctrines always surround us. The worst part is we start to believe them and let them control our lives.

I'll go through the false doctrines we hear from other Christians and break those down with scripture.

My main goal for this section is to break the mindset that's plagued many of us. It's the reason for a lot of issues and problems we face today. Mindset has a lot to do with who and where we are in life. If we can break our old mindset, we can build a new one to drive us forward.

Section Two: Building the Right Mindset

In Matthew 9:17 we read, "People don't pour new wine into old wineskins; they pour new wine into new wineskins, and both are preserved." This is relevant to our mindset. After breaking the bad mindset, our next step is to build the correct one. We first need to remove all of the false teachings and ideas so we can make room for all the correct ones. We need to understand that we live in a time when we see a *lack* more than abundance.

In this section, I'll show how to think in abundance, and by doing so, you'll attract more into all aspects of your life.

I'll also show how important it is to learn about money, how to use it wisely, and why schools don't teach the basic principles we all should know.

I want to help build a strong, abundant mindset and another way of thinking. We need to see the world's abundance and how it can help us be better.

Section Three: The Truth about Money

If you're going to skip ahead, I hope you pause to read this section. It'll give insight into the importance of money, what it really is, what it's for, and how to start living like the wealthy.

But not all money is created equal, and I'll give the good, the bad, and the ugly. Lucky for us, there's more *good* to money than bad or ugliness. We'll learn what the federal reserve isn't telling us, how the wealthy use their money, and how to simulate that for the same results.

Section Four: Being a Good Steward

This section is the *meat* of the book. I'll show how to go from being unwise with money (there's no shame; I was terrible with money) to getting on the right path, clearing up debt, structuring a budget, and investing.

We'll be able to take what we learn in this section, start from scratch, and implement the wisdom right away.

Section four is the most extensive section of the book, but we all need to start somewhere, and for some, we're starting behind with debt, but there is a way out.

* * *

By the end of this book, we'll understand the difference between being *rich* and being *wealthy*. This entire book shows how we can start a foundation so we can be wealthy and not rich.

It's the A to Z guide for getting on the right path to financial literacy. There's so much more to learn when it comes to money and investing. This book, however, gives an excellent leg up. I'll also provide direction on what books to get next to continue on the journey into investing and building a legacy.

INTRODUCTION

The one who plants and the one who waters work together with the same purpose. And both will be rewarded for their own hard work.
—1 Corinthians 3:8 NLT

My wife didn't want to marry me because I was horrible with money, in debt, and didn't have any hope of getting out of debt. That's how bad I was with money. I spent everything I had before my paycheck reached my hands.

Don't get me started on my income tax. I had plans for it before the new year began, only to spend it way differently and on nothing wise. I've never really told my story before, so here goes.

I got married for the first time at a young age of nineteen, and by then, I had two credit cards and a car payment. At times, I worked two jobs, but I'd never made it past the poverty point of income. But that didn't stop me from having the latest phone, a relatively nice car, and the biggest TV I could find at the time to charge with my credit card.

After my divorce, all of my income, which wasn't much (roughly $1,500 a month) was for me, but that didn't help. I was now able to get higher quality stuff, including a convertible sports car and a Harley, and I paid $1,100 for both, including insurance. This doesn't include the debt I incurred at the beginning of adulthood.

I was left with only $400 for gas, debt, and entertainment, which wasn't enough money, so my friends frequently paid for me when I was out with them. (You know who you are.) If you're reading this book, I want to thank you and apologize for all those times. I truly owe you.

So, by the time I started to date my now wife, I was in debt with no plans of getting out. Worse yet, I borrowed her credit to purchase the stuff I wanted. It's no wonder why she didn't want to marry me.

I was beyond repair, horrible with money, and that's putting it graciously.

When we moved in together, it started a whole new set of issues. We rarely fought before, but now living together and sharing finances put a massive strain on our relationship.

I hated fighting about money; it was unbearable stress that kept us awake. It's hard to think, and there's constant worry about it. I even hated payday because I knew there'd be another fight over the inability to pay for something.

Oh, but I couldn't get rid of my Harley, and I needed to have satellite TV.

It didn't take long until I had enough. I didn't know where to start. You'd think that I turned to a Dave Ramsey book, started applying his methods, and it's all better now. But nope, I started reading about money. That's it! I started reading anything about money. If money was in the title of the book, I read it. It wasn't long until I read *Rich Dad Poor Dad*, and it all started to click.

Before that, I learned how to manage money from my parents, and they learned it from their parents. I can only image that they learned it "on the streets." Schools don't teach us about money, so how could I succeed with it if I didn't learn it the *right* way?

Book after book, I gathered all of this knowledge on what money is, how it works, how the government uses it, and how the wealthy use it, which isn't taught to the middle and lower class.

It upset me that *anyone* could be wealthy because no one ever told me that. There are certain principles to follow, and I'm glad I finally learned—it's always better late than never.

Then, the craziest thing happened. When I started to learn those principles, I noticed they all aligned with the Bible.

> If you are born poor it's not your mistake, but if you die poor it's your mistake.
> — Bill Gates

I didn't read the Bible much at that time, but my wife had TBN on every TV. So, there was always a pastor delivering a message on some TV in our house, and they would mention a scripture or something I remembered reading in a business book.

It wasn't long before I started reading the Bible and found the principles to have, make, and be smart with money are all in there.

This isn't about God *wanting us* to be rich. It's about being entrusted with what's been given to us and using it to become financially free. We don't need to live mediocre lives if we're true Christians. We should always strive to be better, care, and provide for others. Stressing out about our bills and money is not how He intended for us to live our lives. We're to leave an inheritance, not go into debt. Most of all, we need to give generously, but when you're running on a tight budget, it's nearly impossible.

I wrote this book for several reasons. One, God put it in my heart to write it. I know there are already a lot of financial books, and Dave Ramsey probably already cornered the market, but mine is different. The difference is I want to open your eyes to how the world works, how the rich use their money, and how scripture dictates how we should use it too.

This book isn't about praying for riches, and this isn't a prosperity gospel book. God is a God of order, and everything He created has a principle and an order for it. The same goes for money. If we follow the principles laid out in this book, we'll be financially free, and some of us may become wealthy.

But wealth comes at a price. No, not our souls, because the problem is not with money; it's with the intentions and the person's heart. When we're wealthy, we have certain obligations we need to carry. I genuinely believe we can be prosperous, and when we are, we do two essential things—love God above all else and love your neighbor as yourself.

Hold on tight. I'm about to shake you up and show you how money works and how you can use it for your benefit.

A wise man should have money in his head,
not in his heart.
—Jonathan Swift

SECTION ONE
BREAKING THE WRONG MENTALITY

*Open my eyes to see the wonderful truths
in your instructions.*

—Psalm 119:18 NLT

CHAPTER 1
THE RENEWING OF OUR MINDS

Do not conform to the pattern of this
world, but be transformed by
the renewing of your mind.

—Romans 12:2

U sually, the state of mind we have when growing up stays with us. I grew up believing we couldn't afford things, and the rich were liars and evil people. Many Christians have the mindset that it's best to be poor. I want to break that mindset. Let's start with a little history of how it affected me.

Richard from Richland

As I grew, I knew three things. My name was Richard. I was born in Richland, WA. I always wanted to be rich. The problem was not wanting; it was how I was told that it was wrong to want that.

I grew up in the Adventist Church, a religion loosely based on some Jewish traditions, including going to church on Saturdays, not eating pork, and other beliefs. Unfortunately, one of the most important things the Adventist religion didn't get from the Jewish tradition was how to handle money—it felt like it was the opposite.

My mom knew I wanted to be rich, so she told me what a lot of God-fearing people still believe. She continuously told me things like, "Rich people are bad, lying, evil men, and you can only be rich if you lie and steal your way to become rich. There is no room for a rich man in heaven. God despises the rich. It's easier for a camel to go through the eye of a needle than for a rich man to enter into heaven. Money is the root of evil." I am sure we have all heard of all, if not some of these.

I know—those are all false beliefs. We'll break down each one of these in later chapters. But I don't blame my mom; she grew up God-fearing and received these doctrines as a child living in poverty herself.

Despite what I learned when I was young, I was determined to be rich and still go to heaven. I thought I would be the first rich man to be kind, honest, and truly go to heaven.

Sadly, I didn't become rich. These false doctrines made it from my mind to my heart and soon became a part of my life. No matter how much I wanted to be rich, deep down inside of me, I felt like it was wrong to want that. It wasn't something I should strive for. And with that, I never made it anywhere. As a matter of fact, up until I was thirty-five years old, I never made more than $18k a year. To give some perspective, in the U.S, if you are in the wealth bracket of $25,750, you are considered to be at the poverty level.

HHS issues poverty guidelines for each household size. For example, the poverty level for a household of four is an annual income of $25,750.[1]

I was taking care of a family of four at the age of thirty-five, and I was way below the poverty line, even with several computer certificates and an associate degree in Biomedical Engineering. So, it wasn't because I didn't go to college.

Even though I had the desire to be rich, I had a stronghold from childhood which affected me well into adulthood. This book is a collection of information over the last five years that have made a difference to me and shown me how to find the abundance in life.

Growing Up

I grew up like any normal kid, except I was an only child until I was seven, so I got the solo attention for a long while. Once my brother was born, it went to him, but I was old enough not to hate him.

One of the only things different from most kids was I loved learning. I was the kid who wanted to read science and biology books. I hated the reading material they gave us for English class. I didn't understand the concept of reading fiction books for fun and not learning anything.

I kept hearing to be successful and rich, we needed to read more. I didn't see the correlation between reading *Charlotte's Web* and me making money. I didn't know some books could teach finances, business, or anything else we wanted to learn. I knew I needed to read, and I also knew what I read was important, but I didn't know the available books. I thought reading textbooks or encyclopedias was wise because I wanted to learn.

I loved learning so much that when I was twelve years old, I bothered my parents to get an encyclopedia set. For those readers younger than twenty-five, an encyclopedia set is a collection of books, each labeled with a letter. That letter signified everything contained within that book. For example, "A" covered aardvarks to Aztecs. It's Google™ in book form.

Back then, its price was about $2–$5k, but we can probably get one now for as little as $500. Living in a poor household, that's why they never purchased it for me. And every time I asked for one, I always got the same answer from my mother. She told me, "Ponte a leer la Biblia." In English, that means, "Go read the Bible." She told me everything I needed to learn and know was in there.

To begin with, I never saw her reading it, and as a twelve-year-old, the Bible was unbelievably boring, especially the King James Version. Plus, I went to church every weekend, so to me, the Bible was a book of rules that didn't want me to be rich.

I never read it, and I strayed away from the church more and more. By my first marriage, I couldn't have been further away from the church or God.

It wasn't until about twenty years later I realized what the Bible *really* is. It's not a book full of rules, and *you can't dos*. It's way more than that.

The Conventional Way

We have a fixed idea of how to make money. When I got out of high school, my thought was the same as others everyone else—go to college, get a good degree, get a high paying job with a degree.

Well, if that isn't the biggest lie of all time, I don't know what is. The best way to get ahead in life isn't to start with $100k in student debt. The school system, from pre-k to high school, is a system to make factory workers and employees.

Don't get me wrong—if you or your child wants to be a professional, doctor, lawyer, etc., then yes, a degree is necessary. (I don't care how much YouTube they watch on performing surgery.) Other than that, going to school for a business degree or graphic design can and will be better learned through experience. It's a Catch-22; we can't get hired because we don't have the experience. We don't have experience because we don't get hired. It's best to skip the middleman and go straight for the experience.

A visit to our kids' school for a day would sound something like this, "Don't talk! Stay in line! Sit quietly! Read this! Do that! No! Do it like this!" And the one I hated the most was, "You have to solve the problem the way I showed you." God forbid we find a better way to solve an algebra problem. If we didn't solve the problem their way, it was wrong, even if we got the same answer in the end.

Is there any wonder why schools don't teach us how *to use* money? Want to know what they teach as far as money is concerned? They teach how to count it! Congratulations, we can now be a cashier or a bank teller. Both of those are respectable jobs, I have been both myself. I'm saying that they only teach you what they want you to know and nothing more.

They don't teach about taxes, investments, the banking system, or anything beneficial. Oh, but we'll need the Pythagorean theory every day of our lives! Anyone care to remember when we learned Columbus discovered America and then later found out it was a bogus lie?

Schools are there to keep us as another cog in the machine. Their system is the same, and they can't have us challenge it. They expect everyone to learn the same and follow the directions and the same methods for solving problems. And if we don't learn it their way, we are considered dumb.

> If you judge a fish by its ability to climb a tree, it will live its whole life believing that it is stupid.
> —Albert Einstein

It was just in 1918 that every state made it required for children to complete high school, and only because they didn't know what to do with so many kids right after eighth grade. So, they put them back into the system!

> *The purpose of the foundation [the General Education Board] was to use the power of money, not to raise the level of education in America, as was widely believed at the time, but to influence the direction of that education ... The object was to use the classroom to teach attitudes that encourage people to be passive and submissive to their rulers. The goal was and is to create citizens who were educated enough for productive work under supervision but not enough to question authority or seek to rise above their class. True education was to be restricted to the sons and daughters of the elite. For the rest, it would be better to produce skilled workers with no particular aspirations other than to enjoy life.*[2]

Comedian George Carlin once said "Governments don't want an intelligent population because people who can think critically can't be controlled. They want a public smart enough to pay taxes but dumb enough to keep voting and electing." He isn't wrong by saying that.

The main point is governments don't want us to think for ourselves because we're easier to control if we don't. They want the general public only to be smart enough to obtain employment, pay taxes, and be a cog in their machine.

So, what we have to do is learn to educate ourselves and not rely on the school system. Maybe we can't beat the system, but we sure can join it.

We are amid wolves; this book will teach how to be wise as serpents and innocent as doves.

* * *

The Instruction Book

The Bible is not a *religious* book or a *rule* book with a bunch of *nos*. That's what I thought also.

Twenty years after my mom told me it has everything I need to know and learn, I finally realized it and started to read it for what it truly is. The Bible is an instruction book of life. Joshua 1:8 tells us to "Keep this Book of the Law always on your lips; meditate on it day and night, so that you may be careful to do everything written in it. Then you will be prosperous and successful."

It's a set of principles laid out for us to use and become successful and prosperous in all we do. It covers all four pillars in life, health, wealth, love, and fulfillment. Now we would need an entire volume set to translate it for each one. But in this book, we will cover wealth.

The teachings in this book will illustrate how the Bible teaches us to be successful and prosperous financially. By the end of this book, you'll have the foundation of what money is, how to use it, how to make it, and, most importantly, how not to fall in love with it.

We've all heard it, and maybe we've even said it. *Money is the root of all evil.* But how true is that? Let's dive into that question a little further and see how we can break that mindset in the next chapter.

Action Step 1

Start thinking of all the false teachings you heard as you grew up and still continue to hear. As you go through this book, come back and write new ones that you want to use to replace the bad ones.

_____

_____

_____

_____

_____

_____

_____

_____

_____

CHAPTER 2
ALL KINDS OF EVIL

*For the love of money is the root of all
kinds of evil. And some people, craving
money, have wandered from the true
faith and pierced themselves with many
sorrows.*

—1 Timothy 6:10 NLT

I magine a world where money is evil. This is one of
the most misquoted verses in the Bible but with good
reason. There are a lot of other scriptures that speak
on the dangers of money and greed. But it never says
physical money is evil.

Money can't be evil—it's inanimate, not good or
evil—it's neutral. It's power, and our choices can make
it good or evil. It's all about the person's intentions.
We may not know what those are, but as Jesus tells us
in Luke 12:7, "the very hairs of your head are all num-
bered." Surely, He will also know what our intentions are.

Of course, there are evil people who use money
wrong and do all kinds of evil. It's not our job to judge,
we are only here to do our part which is already given
to us. Matthew 28:19 says we are here to go and make
disciples of all nations. And we're not to condemn those
who do wrong.

Money Is Evil If You Let It

I'm sure most of us have heard the doctrines that it's
better to be poor than to live a life of riches. And for
the most part, that's true, but God doesn't want us to
live in poverty. What kind of father would want his
children to live in a state of poverty?

But when we hear a scripture like the verse above, it clearly shows Jesus doesn't desire for us to crave or want money. Let's dissect this verse to understand it completely.

First of all, it says, "the *love* of money is the root of *all* kinds of evil." It goes on a little further to say, "*Some* people, craving money, have wandered from the true faith."

They sure don't italicize those in Bible school, do they? What we need to learn from this passage is it's not *money* that's evil but the *love* of it. We need to understand that wealth, although very important, isn't something we can put above our Heavenly Father. "No one can serve two masters. For you will hate one and love the other; you will be devoted to one and despise the other. You cannot serve God and be enslaved to money" (Matthew 6:24 NLT).

I believe this is where the confusion takes place. When viewing these two scriptures with a birds-eye view, money is evil and something we shouldn't want. We can create a false doctrine out of these two scriptures—we shouldn't want money or wealth, and we should live in a state of *just enough*.

But what is enough?

Just Enough Is Not Enough

I heard we didn't have enough, couldn't afford that, or didn't have the money for it my whole life. I grew up poor, and my parents wouldn't let me forget it.

Not only was I poor, but my parents wanted me to be okay with that. They wanted me to accept and embrace it because we were Godly and Christian and had to remain in poverty so we could stay humble.

"Be poor; get a degree; get a good job, but stay in your lane. The middle class is okay, but don't try and be rich. We can only be rich if we lie and cheat our way there."

None of this made any sense to me. Why would God, our Father, wants us to live in a state of not enough?

This rule about a God of lack wasn't a God I wanted to serve. I didn't want to worship a God who wanted us to struggle and be in poverty.

I'm sure I wasn't alone, living paycheck to paycheck, unable to afford certain things, or able to help the people in need. We have a lot of family members below the poverty line, and we couldn't help them. How is this okay?

These relatives had less than I ever did. I'm talking about dirt floors and aluminum roofs. If it rained, no one slept.

As a child, I remember making a fire pit in the middle of the living room because it was cold outside. I also remember helping my mom walk to an out-house in the middle of the night because there wasn't indoor plumbing.

That's not how we were supposed to live. Did it make me humble? Yes, it did. And for that, I'm grateful. But it also made me realize we shouldn't stay there.

> May he give you the desire of your heart and make all your plans succeed.
> —Psalms 20:4

How can I help anyone get out of a hole if I'm standing right next to them? We need to be blessed to be a blessing, and it took me a long while to find out for myself that was what our God wants from us.

The Problem with Contentment

Before Paul says the love of money is the root of all kinds of evil, he says, "But if we have food and clothing, we will be *content* with that. People who want to get rich fall into temptation and a trap and into many foolish and harmful desires that plunge men into ruin and destruction" (1 Timothy 6:8).

A Google search on contentment in the Bible will lead to Bible Money Matters by Peter Anderson. "Contentment can't be found in God's creation or in things like people, possessions, or money."[3]

Is it any wonder why Christians teach it's better to be poor? We fail to realize two things. First, contentment means to be in a state of peaceful happiness. Two, Paul's teaching shows us we're unable to reach a state of peaceful happiness with worldly wealth, and those trying to be happy through obtaining money can and will fall.

Contentment doesn't mean settling with what we have and staying stagnant. It means having peaceful happiness in any situation, but we should always strive to be better than the person we were yesterday. It's the constant pursuit of progress that keeps us living. Ever notice that after retirement, there is faster rate of declining? The average lifespan of a person in a nursing home is eight months. Can you believe that? Ever wonder why? Because all progress stops.

My grandfather was a hard-working man all his life. After his retirement, there was a time he lived with my parents, and you could not see the man sitting down. He was always doing something. As he got older, everyone told him to stop working so much. He finally listened and started getting sick and was placed in a nursing home. Shortly thereafter, he passed away. While he was working, there was progress and momentum; he was strong and kept going. In the famous words of Tom Petty, "You never slow down, you never grow old." Once he slowed down, everything else did too.

We are supposed to grow and stretch to our limits; it's okay to want to have a good and prosperous future. It's what keeps moving us forward. Jeremiah 29:11 tells us, "For I know the plans I have for you," declares the Lord, "plans to prosper you and not to harm you, plans to give you hope and a future."

Sounds like an Oxymoron . . .

Now, how do we do that? How do we go from thinking that money is not evil to thinking we can prosper? How do we go from not loving money to having money?

Trust me; these were all questions I had. And the answer is more straightforward than we can imagine.

Be thankful—that's the real trick. We have to be grateful for everything we have. Being grateful won't put us in a state of *just enough*, and it certainly won't make us feel like we aren't content. It's one of the most powerful things we can start putting into practice. 1 Timothy 4:4 tells us, "For everything God created is good, and nothing is to be rejected if it is received with thanksgiving."

One of the main issues we face when we don't have enough is wanting more and not being thankful for the things we already have. We're unable to see God for who He is and begin to feel like the only way to feel better is to have more. We get stuck in a state of lack.

We start craving more money and possessions, and we get into this spiral of seeing the things we don't have. We want more! At times, this can make us do things we wouldn't normally do—sometimes, we do downright evil things.

Now, does *the love of money is the root of all kinds of evil* make sense?

To be thankful for what we have every day, every hour, and in any situation or social class we're in will generate the feeling of contentment and peaceful happiness we can't get anywhere else.

We went over how we look at money and how thanksgiving and contentment all play a vital role in our success. In the following chapter, we'll see how much more the words we speak give life or take it away.

* * *

I pray that you all put your shoes way under the
bed at night so that you gotta get on your knees
in the morning to find them. And while you're
down there, thank God for grace and mercy and
understanding. We all fall short of glory;
we all got plenty.
—Denzel Washington

Action Step 2

This particular action step is a big one. No matter where you are in your life, you need to be thankful for what you have. This may seem hard in some cases. I know there were times in my life that it was hard to think of things I was thankful for. I urge you to come up with as many as you can. If you can't think of any, simply start with giving thanks that you are alive. Do this everyday, and eventually, you will find more and more things to be thankful for.

This is a big step, so don't skip it. Write down what you are thankful for, repeat it every day, add to it, and always be grateful for even the smallest things that we might sometimes take for granted.

I am thankful for

_____

_____

_____

_____

_____

_____

CHAPTER 3
WORD OF LIFE

For the mouth speaks
what the heart is full of.

—Luke 6:45

To start breaking the wrong mindset we have developed over the years, we first need to start watching our mouths. What we speak with our outer voice and believe with our inner voice has a strong influence over what we get out of life.

It shapes who we are and determines where we're going. If we control what we speak, we can start controlling much more. Words give us life. In this chapter, we'll go over several different stories and change what we say so we can experience true riches.

Sticks and Stones

Studies have shown that by the time we are thirty-five years old, our daily lives live on a subconscious level. Joe Dispenza says, "95% of who you are by the time you are 35 years old is a set of memorized behaviors and emotional reactions that create and identity subconsciously."[4] Everything we do—how we act and how we react—are programmed traits we have established throughout our lives. This, of course, includes how we speak.

Every time we speak, we're either speaking life or death, a blessing, or a curse. This is why they call it curse words because you're cursing yourself every time you say them. We underestimate how the power of words affect our lives and how much they control it.

For those born before the 1990s, we grew up with sayings such as "sticks and stones will break my bones, but words will never hurt me." I say, let's continue this practice in our lives when others speak to us. Because while we can't control what others say or do, we can control ourselves.

Let me repeat that, we can't control what others say or do; we can only control our actions in what we say, what we do, and how we react to outside circumstances. If we don't like a situation, we can remove ourselves from it, We can't change those around us, but we can change those around us.

We can't, however, remove ourselves from ourselves, and self-talk is one of the most destructive forces. What we say out loud and what we think has the power to influence our lives.

Very Bad Words

In my home—like most homes—my kids know there are bad words, and they're not allowed to speak them. But at the top of that list are some added ones I won't tolerate no matter how old they are.

- "I can't."
- "It's hard."
- "I'll never be able."
- "I don't know."

These are among the worst words you can't speak. They limit the mind and hinder the spirit. The only time my kids can say "I can't" is if it's followed by "yet." They know failure is always an option; quitting isn't.

Kids aren't the only ones who struggle with this. It took me a long time to remove those words out of *my* vocabulary. Possibly one of the hardest ones to remove is one my parents drove into me all the time, and I'm sure most of us have said or thought it more often than we care to remember. *We can't afford it.*

Can we follow that with *yet?* Sure, we can go one step further and consider, *What can we do to afford it?* Saying it this way will stretch the mind to think and forces us to come up with solutions instead of stopping us from achieving goals, dreams, or desired outcomes.

Limiting words have a strong psychological effect on us. When we use the word *but*, we discredit anything we previously said. *I want to tithe, but I have too many bills.* Are our minds focused on wanting to tithe or on taking care of the bills?

Stop with, *I should,* and replace it with: *I will.* Yes, I threw that one in there too. *I should start watching how I speak.*

"Words are the most powerful force available to humanity. We can choose to use this force constructively with words of encouragement or with words of despair to bring destruction. Words have energy and power with the ability to help, to heal, to hinder, to hurt, to harm, to humiliate and humble."[5]

We need to be mindful of what we say out loud because we also internalize it. Our minds will pick it up, and it'll either build us up or bring us down. Remember, we're always listening to ourselves. Even simple things like *"I only get bills in the mail," "My bank account is always overdrafted," "I already spent all my paycheck,"* can have a debilitating effect.

Not only should we watch what we say for our sake, but we should also be sure to build people up. Words of encouragement and other kind words can make a difference in our lives and the lives of those around us. Proverbs is full of verses about the benefits of life-giving words.

Such as: "Kind words are like honey-sweet to the soul and healthy for the body" (Proverbs 16:24 NLT). And "Your own soul is nourished when you are kind, but you destroy yourself when you are cruel" (Proverbs 11:17 NLT). Solomon, the wisest man, knew the power of words and the effects it can have.

> A person's words can be life-giving water; words of true wisdom are as refreshing as a bubbling brook.
> — Proverbs 18:4 NLT

Bringing out the Beauty in Someone

The story of Johnny Lingo is a short movie based on a short story by Patricia McGerr. It's a tale of a clever but honest and well-liked Polynesian trader. Lingo comes to one island to bargain for a wife and is smitten by a native named Mahana. Her neighbors, her family, and even her father considered Mahana to be of little value. She was raised that way and heard that every day of her life.

On this island, a person who wanted a wife was given one depending on the worth of their cows. Word quickly spread that Mahana was the desire in Lingo's heart, and they began to say her father would be lucky to see one cow. Mahana felt her worth was justified mainly because that's what she'd been told her whole life. Her father began the bargaining by asking for three cows because he thought he'd at least get one cow out of the deal.

The bargaining began, and Islanders laughed at the notion that it started at three cows. Their anticipation grew as they waited to see what Lingo's counteroffer would be. Lingo considered and said three cows were many, "But not enough for Mahana!" He offered the price of *eight* cows for her hand in marriage. Her father, shaken by his offer, agreed before he could change his mind.

The next day, Lingo brought the cows and married Mahana that night while her father delighted in his newfound prosperity. Later, Johnny and Mahana left the island only to return years later to visit. Everyone was surprised by Mahana's beauty and lively spirit. But Mahana's father was in disbelief and began accusing Lingo of conning him and only giving him eight cows for a woman who was worth ten cows. He asked how she transformed into the gorgeous woman standing before him.

Her real worth was not on what others saw but in what she saw in herself. The problem was that all her life she heard she was ugly and undesirable, even by her loved ones. She heard it so often she began to believe them, and it limited her inner self-worth, which affected her outer appearance. Lingo knew she was special; he saw her for who she truly was before she was broken. With words of love and affirmation about how beautiful and precious she is, she was able to break her limiting mindset and become the person she truly was.

Proverbs 15:4 tells us, "Gentle words bring life and health; a deceitful tongue crushes the spirit." Now we know words have the power to do great and wonderful things or cause destruction. We need to be very mindful of what we're speaking as we either speak life or death.

We must understand the power of words to bring life to a person. Remember, in the beginning, God *spoke,* and everything was created. The enemy knows all he has to do is corrupt our speech, which allows him to control everything else. In later chapters, we'll talk about how he can do this.

For now, understand that what we speak greatly influences everything around us. We either speak words of life and abundance, or we speak words of death and lack. Simple things in our everyday speech like "My feet are killing me," or "I'm dying to see that movie," or "This is boring me to death," or "I can't afford that," or "It's too expensive" all have the same effect. They all bring death or lack to fruition.

Remove these words from everyday speech, and things will start moving toward our desired goals. In Chapter 4, I'll go over one of the most famous parables people use to show how the rich won't be able to enter heaven. I'll explain how easy it is for a camel to go through the eye of a needle.

Action Step 3

We all have words or phrases that we need to get rid of. As for me, I had a couple that I needed to get rid of: "You're killing me," and "It's too expensive."

Being aware of what we say most often will help remove those negative phrases from our vocabulary. Take some time and write down which ones you use most often. Feel free to come back if you discover more. On the opposite side, write down what phrase you can replace it with.

Wrong Phrase   Replacement Phrase

_____   _____

_____   _____

_____   _____

_____   _____

_____   _____

_____   _____

_____   _____

CHAPTER 4

CAMEL THROUGH THE EYE OF A NEEDLE

*I'll say it again—it is easier for a camel to
go through the eye of a needle than for a
rich person to enter the Kingdom of God!*

—Matthew 19:24 NLT

T his verse is forever engraved in my head. As I said
earlier, my mom has always been a God-fearing
woman, and so when I said I wanted to be rich, she
would *Bible* me with this scripture.

I thought I could do it. I could be rich and go to
heaven. There had to be a way!

The good news is there is a way. And I'm here to
show you.

For most of us, we've probably heard this parable,
but I'd like to go through it again. Bear with me as we
go through the parable, so we can shed some light on
how we can get a camel through the eye of a needle.

Right before this parable, Matthew 19:13 (NIV)
introduces a foundation from which we need to start.

The Little Children and Jesus

*Then people brought little children to Jesus for Him
to place His hands on them and pray for them. But
the disciples rebuked them. Jesus said, 'Let the little
children come to me, and do not hinder them, for the
kingdom of heaven belongs to such as these.' When He
had placed His hands on them, He went on from there.*

The Rich and the Kingdom of God

Just then, a man came up to Jesus and asked, 'Teacher, what good thing must I do to get eternal life?' 'Why do you ask me about what is good?' Jesus replied. 'There is only One who is good. That is God. If you want to enter life, keep the commandments.' 'Which ones?' he inquired. Jesus replied, 'You shall not murder, you shall not commit adultery, you shall not steal, you shall not give false testimony, honor your father and mother, and love your neighbor as yourself.' 'All these I have kept,' the young man said. 'What do I still lack?' Jesus answered, 'If you want to be perfect, go, sell your possessions and give to the poor, and you will have treasure in heaven. Then come, follow me.' When the young man heard this, he went away sad because he had great wealth. Then Jesus said to his disciples, 'Truly I tell you, it is hard for someone who is rich to enter the kingdom of heaven. Again I tell you, it is easier for a camel to go through the eye of a needle than for someone who is rich to enter the kingdom of God.' When the disciples heard this, they were greatly astonished and asked, 'Who then can be saved?' Jesus looked at them and said, 'With man this is impossible, but with God all things are possible.'

How to Get a Camel through the Eye of a Needle

Now that we've read the entire parable, let's go through it and see why Jesus would say a rich man won't enter the kingdom of God. It took me twenty-five years to read this for myself and others to explain it to me in various ways. This shows we need to understand things for ourselves and ask multiple people.

We start in the first parable with the children. Children were running around and wanted to get to Jesus, but the disciples stopped them until Jesus spoke and said, "Let the little children come to me and do not hinder them, for the kingdom of heaven belongs to such as these."

This single verse sets the pace for the rest of the teachings. What Jesus is saying is we need to have childlike faith and heart. And we know this because previously in Matthew 18:13, He said, "Truly I tell you, unless you change and become like little children, you will never enter the kingdom of heaven." Before that, in Psalms 116:6, He said, "The Lord protects those of childlike faith."

Right after this, a rich man comes to Jesus, starts questioning him, and has a conversation.

> **Rich Man:** "Teacher, what good thing must I do to get eternal life?"

I'm more than sure most of us would have asked this question. This guy wanted an easy answer. He wanted to make sure he'd enter the kingdom. Jesus knew the man's intentions. And being a rabbi, Jesus answered with a question and a basic answer to test the man.

> **Jesus:** "Why do you ask me about what is good? There is only One who is good. That is God. If you want to enter life, keep the commandments."

He stops anything from going further and says no one is good except God. I love how Jesus replies when asked questions. He starts with a question, putting the guy in his place, and then gives him the most basic answer. The rabbis answered in the form of a riddle to allow the other person to think and come up with a conclusion. A true teacher makes us think, and Jesus is a perfect example of this. But of course, like most of us, the man wanted to know specifics.

Rich Man: "Which ones?"

However, he asked it unwisely. Which ones? At this point, Jesus knew what he was up to. The rich man wanted to know which one he needed to follow so he could do that one and not worry about not getting into heaven. Jesus strung him along and continued. I admire His patience.

> **Jesus:** "You shall not murder, you shall not commit adultery, you shall not steal, you shall not give false testimony, honor your father and mother, and love your neighbor as yourself."

> **Rich Man:** "All these I have kept. What do I still lack?"

At this point, the guy thinks he's kept all the commandments and is perfect. But Jesus knows what's truly in his heart. So, he presses on and hits the man right where he knows he's flawed—his wallet.

> **Jesus:** "If you want to be perfect, go, sell your possessions and give to the poor, and you will have treasure in heaven. Then come, follow me."

This answer has got to be the most beautiful in-your-face reply. If the rich man was perfect and followed all commandments, then surely, he'd have obeyed the last one Jesus mentioned. "Love your neighbor as yourself," and then he said, "Come follow me."

That is why Jesus told him to sell his possessions, give to the poor, and follow Him. If he did obey all commandments, then he'd have been able to do that. After all, that is the greatest commandment of all. Matthew 22:37-40 tells us, "Love the Lord your God with all your heart and with all your soul and with all your mind. This is the first and greatest commandment. And the second is like it: Love your neighbor as yourself. All the Law and the Prophets hang on these two commandments."

There are two things to point out to eliminate any fuzziness:

1) "Sell all your possessions and follow me" equals "Love the Lord Your God above all things."

2) "Give to the poor" equals "Love your neighbor as yourself."

To drive this point home, the man didn't love the Lord first. If he had, the man would've been okay giving up all his possessions on top of following Jesus. Lastly, he didn't love his neighbor as himself, or he would've given to the poor and ones in need. With that, the guy knew he didn't follow all commandments and left. NKJV says, "for he had many possessions." He had, but he was unwilling to give it up for his neighbor, and more importantly, to follow Jesus.

But wait, there's more. This is where the parable gets even better.

Jesus: "Truly I tell you, it is hard for someone who is rich to enter the kingdom of heaven. Again I tell you, it is easier for a camel to go through the eye of a needle than for someone who is rich to enter the kingdom of God."

Here is where the rubber meets the road. Jesus clearly states that it's *hard* for someone rich to enter the kingdom of heaven. Camel meet needle. When the disciples heard this, they were greatly astonished.

Disciples: "Who then can be saved?"

Having heard this, it freaked out the disciples. And here comes the kicker.

Jesus: "With man this is impossible, but with God, all things are possible."

Like the rich man, we try to see or figure out how to get into heaven. But the reality is, all things are possible with God. However, we need to seek him first.

Let's come full circle. Matthew 19:14 tells us, "Let the little children come to me, and do not hinder them, for the kingdom of heaven belongs to such as these." The problem is we see everything through adult eyes. Like the rich man, we want to buy our way out of things, which is why a rich man won't be able to enter heaven.

You can't buy your way into heaven!

Is there any wonder why Jesus said it's hard? The problem isn't *being rich*; the problem is seeing money as your savior. This is why the love of money is the root of all kinds of evil because we start loving what it can do for us here on earth. The more money you have, the more you can purchase and the more things you can do.

We forget and try to buy our way into the kingdom of God. 1 John 2:15 (NKJV) says, "Do not love the world or the things in the world. If anyone loves the world, the love of the Father is not in him." John 18:36 says, "My kingdom is not of this world."

Oh, it gets better! In the next chapter, I'll explain what I failed to realize, which might be the most eye-opening part.

CHAPTER 5
LIVESTOCK, SILVER, AND GOLD

King Solomon was richer and wiser than
any other king in the world.

—2 Chronicles 9:22

Everyone says it's better to live a poor life and a rich man won't enter the kingdom of God. But no one ever considers super-wealthy men in the Bible like Abraham, Joseph, Isaac, Jacob, King David, King Solomon, Job, Zacchaeus, Hezekiah, and on and on.

They were wealthy because *God made them wealthy*, and on top of that, they all entered the kingdom of God.

With so much focus given to the poor, we don't stop and look at the wealth of these men who also found favor in God's eyes. Each of these men had certain qualities that caused God and God's people to favor them. They also knew how to use money as a tool, and not one of them were ever greedy for more.

There's so much to learn from these men that I can't possibly fit it into a chapter or two. The focus of my next book is to focus on each man to learn from them. Like the book title, *7 Habits of Highly Effective People* by Stephen Covey, in the same way, the working title for my next book is, *Habits of the Richest Men in the Bible*, so keep an eye out for it.

Blessed by the Lord

The Lord favored these men because they praised and worshipped Him when no one else did. They remained faithful in their actions, even when others turned their backs on the Lord.

Were they rich before? Who knows? But one thing for sure is that their wealth continued. God blessed them with land, cattle, silver, and gold.

All the accounts of these men showed their extraordinary natures. Not only did they follow God's instructions, but they also did everything good in the Lord's eyes. And because of that, God blessed them.

Far beyond that, they were never greedy and gave freely. They never had a love for money. Here are only a couple of examples to illustrate my point.

Abraham

In Genesis 13:2, we read, "Abram was very rich in livestock, silver, and gold."

Abraham was the first person ever to be mentioned as a wealthy man in the Bible. He was the father of all nations and the man that God made a covenant with. Abraham was wealthy beyond belief, and yet he was as humble as they come.

There is so much we can all learn from Abraham. He didn't hesitate, but instead, he quickly responded to God's commands, was a servant to others, and praised God for everything. Because his faith was unwavering, he is also known as the father of faith. He had a level of faith that we can all learn from. He didn't stop to question or doubt. Often, we stop because of either doubt or fear; we question whether something will work. We always need to have faith and look toward God as our provider and know that we are successful in all that we do because ultimately, it's His will be done.

King David

King David was the man after God's own heart. One thing that stands out about King David is no matter what circumstance, bad or good, he never lost sight of God.

Even when he won a war, he gave all glory to God. Multiple times in the Bible, he says, "You Lord have won the war." He never once says that *he* had the victory or how he became king. He gave God all the credit.

Later in this book, we will discuss how God gives us the things we have. All good comes directly from Him, yet we consumed with "I."

I got a raise. I got the job. I got first place. I graduated. Okay, you get the point.

It's always good to celebrate your victories, but it's even better when you give credit where credit is due.

King Solomon

One of my favorites is the richest man in the Bible who needs no introduction—King Solomon.

What can I say about King Solomon that people don't already know? This man, when asked by God what he wanted, answered "wisdom and discernment."

Let's take a step back for a second. If we were asked by God what we wanted, what would we say? Most of us have a Christmas list of things we'd want! Would wisdom be on that list? Be honest—God's watching.

With everything he could've asked for, he asked for and received wisdom, and God put the cherry on top with all the wealth and riches the man could ever ask for. He put his wants aside and asked not for wisdom to know how to be a better king for his people and discernment to judge them fairly. He looked beyond himself and wanted better for others.

Because of his humble and heartfelt request, God gave him so much more. To this day, he is still considered the wisest, richest man who ever lived.

Now we can appreciate the fact that money isn't evil. It's not evil to have it, want it, or need it. We need to understand what it is and how to use it. In the next section, we'll build the proper mindset, and I'll show you exactly how to use it so it's a tool to *create* rather than to *destroy*.

Job

Most of us know the story of Job and how he was a rich landowner with livestock that had everything. His family, his finances, and his health were secured because of this ability to trust and worship God.

Perhaps what's so great about this man is that he had no clue about the conversation had between God and Satan. God lifted his protection from him and gave Satan full rein over Job so long

> Then the Lord said to Satan, "Have you considered my servant Job? There is no one on earth like him; he is blameless and upright, a man who fears God and shuns evil."
> —Job 1:8

as he didn't take his life. Everything was taken away from him, but he never let it affect his relationship with God. So many of us have hiccups in life, and it stops us in our tracks. Getting laid off from our job or an injury will leave us feeling helpless. We must remember, like Job, that we have a much higher power looking over us. Staying the course with our faith, we can overcome more than what the enemy throws at us.

* * *

Now that we have broken the incorrect mindset and false doctrines, in the next section we will learn how to build the correct mindset. We will learn how to see abundance in the world and the first sin that started us on the wrong path.

SECTION TWO
BUILDING THE CORRECT MINDSET

Fix your thoughts on what is true, and honorable, and right, and pure, and lovely, and admirable. Think about things that are excellent and worthy of praise.

—Philippians 4:8 NLT

CHAPTER 6
HAVE LIFE ABUNDANTLY

The thief comes only to steal and kill and destroy. I came that they may have life and that they may have it abundantly.

—John 10:10 NKJV

In this chapter, we'll start building the correct mindset. We're all in a world that sees lack or not enough in everything. But from here on forward, I'll show how we can see the abundance.

Seek the Kingdom

Here's the first thing to realize. Everything on this earth and forever is abundant, including money. You shouldn't crave it, chase it, or hoard it. This'll be a repeating theme in this book.

Gary Vaynerchuk says, "People are chasing cash, not happiness. When you chase money, you're going to lose. You're just going to."

Luke 12:31 (NLT) tells us, "Seek the Kingdom of God above all else, and He will give you everything you need." God gives us a direct promise when he tells us to seek His kingdom first. He clearly states He'll provide us with everything we need. Does that include a Porsche with the beachside property? Probably not. But it does mean we'll be taken care of, and He has taken full responsibility for our needs.

Matthew 6:31-32 (NLT) says, "So don't worry about these things, saying, 'What will we eat? What will we drink? What will we wear?'" These things dominate the thoughts of unbelievers, but our heavenly Father already knows *all our needs*.

That doesn't mean we can sit on our couch, eat Cheetos, and everything will come to us. We need to get up and do something, to work to make anything function as we read in James 2:26 (NLT). "Just as the body is dead without breath, so also faith is dead without good works."

All the Bible's greatest people had to apply work to receive any of the blessings or promises. Abraham had to get up and go. Moses had to raise his staff. David had to go into battle. All the disciples and apostles had to put in the work. Nothing was given to them until they put their sweat equity and faith in along with it. *Work has to be applied to get anything in return.* It's a physical law!

$$P=W/t$$
Power equals work over time

The Source of It All

We must start considering the source of everything. It's hard not to see the scarcity sometimes. We look at our bank account, our fridge, and even the gas tank and see what we *don't* have. I'm not saying we need to be Mister or Misses Glass Half-Full, but we need to start looking at everything from a place of abundance.

In the last section, we talked about how powerful words are. And this primarily includes self-talk. The mind can play tricks on us if we don't capture our thoughts. Our real source has the potential to do all things.

Let's break down the first days of creation. In Genesis 1:3 (Day 1), "And God said, 'Let there be light,' and there was light." In Genesis 1:14 NLT (Day 4), "And God said, 'Let lights appear in the sky to separate the day from the night.'" So, day one, God said, "Let there be light," but on day four, he created the sun.

This shows what we see as being our *light* here on this planet is not the true source of light. As humans, we see the sun as our source of light, like we see our bank accounts as our source of providing. God doesn't need our bank account, and he doesn't require our stock portfolio or savings account.

We need to realize there was light before the sun was even created. God is our source of *everything*. He doesn't need the sun for light, and he surely doesn't require a bank account to provide for us.

Why All This?

I said all of this to create awareness that our mindset is a massive contribution to how we perceive the world. 90% of everything that happens in our life is all due to our mindset.

Our humanity tends to always look at the lack and creates our lack mentality.

For anyone who's taken a Physics class, energy isn't created and can't be destroyed. Also, a high energy source can't occupy a low energy source.

We need to have high energy to receive high energy. Our circumstances greatly influence our mindsets, and if we don't learn to control that, we'll always be in a lower energy field.

By understanding the higher power of God is and forever will be on our side, we can stand firm that He is our dependable source, and He is the highest of energies.

In His Image

Then, in Genesis 1:26 (NLT), God said, "Let us make human beings in our image, to be like us."

If God made us in His image, not only do we have high energy, but we're also the first thing God mentions He is: a creator.

Genesis 1:1 says, "In the beginning, *God created* the heavens and the earth."

At this point, we should now know two key points we didn't know before. We're high energy, and we're creators. We have the power to create a life of high energy.

No matter where we're from, how we grew up, or our current circumstances, we have all the abilities to see our way out. This ability has been given to us from the very beginning. We have to unleash it. And it all starts with our mindsets—ask Oprah, Tony Robbins, Steve Harvey, Walt Disney, and even Hezekiah.

Hezekiah was the son of King Ahaz; King Ahaz was one of the worst kings in Israel. He worshiped other gods and let the entire city get demolished. His household wasn't any better; he treated his wife and kids just as bad. We can see Hezekiah had everything against him—a horrible upbringing and even worse circumstances around him.

When his father, King Ahaz, passed, he was put in command. The very first thing he did was rebuild the temple of God. He didn't let his surroundings dictate what he was supposed to do or create.

Shortly after that, the city started to rebuild and come back to life. By the end of his reign, he was known as one of the best kings to have ever lived. He accomplished all of this regardless of how and where he grew up.

We have the power to do the same. Focus your attention first on God, and everything else follows.

Someone once told me, "The sun shines for everyone." This is true for all things. There's plenty to go around, but we seem to focus on what we *don't* have. Unfortunately, that's human nature, and it's been happening since the Garden of Eden.

How ingrained is this thinking? It was one of our first sins, just before Adam and Eve ate the forbidden fruit. In Chapter 7, we'll discover how easy it is for our minds to adapt to a negative mindset of lack.

CHAPTER 7
OF EVERY TREE FREELY EAT

*The Lord God placed the man in the
Garden of Eden to tend and watch over it.*

—Genesis 2:15

One person I follow and learn a lot from is Myron Golden. If you don't know him, I would suggest you look him up on any social media and follow him. He is a wonderful human being and a great teacher of God and his principles. There are many things in this book that I learned from him. When you follow him, you will see how he brings them to life.

One example that he preaches is the story of Adam and Eve and how they were given everything and lacked nothing. Yet they were easily deceived into focusing on what they *didn't* have. Our thoughts and speech, as we learned, can have a powerful effect on us.

Let's go to the beginning of it all and pay close attention to how it all unfolds.

The Fall

Most of us know the story of Adam and Eve and the fall. However, we're still committing one of the most basic sins that started it all. In the beginning, there were two trees located right smack in the middle of the Garden of Eden as we learn in Genesis 2:9. "The Lord God made all kinds of trees grow out of the ground—trees that were pleasing to the eye and good for food. In the middle of the garden were the tree of life and the tree of the knowledge of good and evil."

One of those trees came with a *strict* rule for Adam and Eve to follow. They were told not to eat from that tree, or it would cause death. In Genesis 2:16-17 (NKJV), "And the Lord God commanded the man, saying, 'Of every tree of the garden you may freely eat; but of the tree of the knowledge of good and evil you shall not eat, for in the day that you eat of it you shall surely die.'"

Let's take a couple of steps back and see the first part of that verse "Of *every* tree of the garden you may *freely* eat."

God said, "Of *every*; you may *freely* eat." These are both words of abundance. From the very start, He's given us abundance. But what does the enemy do? He tricks us and strips us of that abundance! How does he do it? He places the thought in our minds, which gives us a limiting mindset.

First, the enemy places the thought in our minds, then he strategically places an unwanted word or replaces it so that it's easy for us to take it and run with it. As the story continues in Genesis 3:1, we see how easily we're swayed. "Now the serpent was more cunning than any beast of the field which the Lord God had made. And he said to the woman, 'Has God indeed said, "You shall not eat of every tree of the garden?"'"

Did you see the subtlety? All he did was remove the world *freely* and made the question into a negative one.

In Genesis 3:2, we hear the famous last words: "And the woman said to the serpent, 'We may eat the fruit of the trees of the garden.'" The woman removed the word *every*. Without the words of abundance, all we have is the lack. She even adds to the lack in the following verse of Genesis 3:3 (NKJV), "But of the fruit of the tree which *is* in the midst of the garden, God has said, 'You shall not eat it, nor shall you touch it, lest you die.'"

Now, she added more things not to do. *Don't eat it; don't touch it.*

It's a simple story with a powerful message that still plagues us. Like Adam and Eve walked through all the abundance the Garden of Eden offered only to get to the one tree they couldn't eat from, we, too, pass by all of the abundances and focus on the lack.

Where focus goes, energy goes.
—Tony Robbins

We continually focus on our lack—depleting bank accounts and all the things we want and don't have. We completely fail to see all the things we *do* have.

There's an incredible thing that happens when we're thankful for all the things we have and focus on abundance. The scarcity mentality ceases to exist. It's even better when we start to give thanks for the things we want as though we already have them. 2 Corinthians 5:7 (NKJV) tells us "For we walk by faith, not by sight."

If we focus on the things we don't have, then we consume our lives with lack, which gives power to the lack. Have you ever thought about these things? *I always get bills in the mail. I'm always getting overdraft charges from my bank.* It's a horrible self-fulfilling prophecy. The more you say it, the more it will come to fruition.

More Than Enough

Another popular story in the Bible took place when Jesus went to a remote area purposely to spend time alone. But as soon as people found out, crowds gathered around him.

After a while of listening to his teachings, the disciples told him it was getting late and to send everyone away so they could get food for themselves.

But Jesus said, "That isn't necessary; you feed them." Matthew 14:16

"But we have only five loaves of bread and two fish!" they answered.

"Bring them here," he said.

Then, he told the people to sit down on the grass. He took the five loaves and two fish, and looking up to heaven, he gave thanks and broke the loaves. Then, he gave the bread to the disciples, who distributed it to the people.

Notice that before Jesus had enough for everyone, He gave thanks for what He had. It may have only been five loaves and two fish and needed to feed 5,000 people, but He gave thanks for what He had.

The disciples were able to give everyone food. Interestingly, He was able to feed 5,000 people, but He was also able to provide them with as much as they wanted to consume. They ate until they were satisfied. Afterward, the disciples picked up twelve baskets of leftovers!

As you can see, He's not a God of just enough or barely enough. He is a God of *more than enough!*

Please understand, changing our mindset from scarcity to abundance can significantly influence our lives and those around us. We can't let the negative input of others into our minds. Instead, we need to surround ourselves with people who'll lift us.

Who Your Friends Are

Don't be deceived. 1 Corinthians 15:33 (NKJV) tells us, "Evil company corrupts good habits." I know it's easier said than done. That's why we need to be around others who feel the same way, and we need to invest in ourselves continually.

Growing up, my mom would always tell me, "tell me who your friends are, and I will tell you who you are." At the time, I thought this was the most bogus thing ever. Little did I know how true this was. Our social circle not only defines who we are, but it will also make us better or worse. If we surround ourselves with people that don't try and better themselves or don't have ambition, we won't either. If we hang around five poor minded individuals, we will be the sixth.

My life started to take a giant leap forward once I changed the circle of people I surrounded myself with. My Facebook feed became more positive and encouraging right after I unfriended anyone that posted something negative, yes, that includes close friends and family. I don't have time or energy to entertain negativity or hate, and neither should you. I wouldn't have any mercy; if anyone posted anything negative, I would unfriend them on the spot. Even when accepting people's request, I would take the time to look at their timeline. If I didn't like what I saw, I wouldn't accept their request. We need to be very selective in the people we allow in our circle.

One of the most extraordinary things that happened to me was finding like-minded people like myself in my area and hanging out with them. I became good friends with them, and now they are and will always be a part of my life. They were a significant contributing factor in upgrading my mindset and level of where I was. Even Jesus Christ surrounded himself with like-minded individuals. Solomon tells us in Proverbs 27:17, "As iron sharpens iron, so does one person sharpen another."

This is one of the primary factors of success. It's as simple as going to meetup.com and picking an interest. It will show groups meeting up in the area regarding hobbies or interests. There are also conferences we can go to, and even Facebook is a great way to connect with like-minded people. I talk to people worldwide with the same goals and ambitions I do via social media. So don't be shy and go out and make friends that will level you up. Remember to do the same as scripture says "Therefore encourage one another and build one another up, just as you are doing." (1 Thessalonians 5:11)

* * *

This is not exactly an action step so much as it is a suggestion. Take the time to go through your social media accounts and see if you can change what you see on your timeline. I don't want to tell you to remove people, but I want you to be aware that the people we associate with most will determine where we are in life and how we think. In the next chapter, we will discuss how important it is to invest in ourselves.

CHAPTER 8
WORTH MORE THAN SILVER & GOLD

If you need wisdom, ask our generous God,
and he will give it to you. He will not
rebuke you for asking.

—James 1:5 NLT

Once we realize the world is full of abundance, we can grab hold of *how*. And like any other chapter in this book, I'll always go back to Proverbs. The wisest, richest man in the Bible, King Solomon, wrote the book of Proverbs. His teachings on what he learned and how to deal with difficulties throughout life are summed up in Proverbs. But the greatest lesson he spoke about was wisdom. He knew true riches came from being wise.

When I was young, my mom always told me the story of King Solomon, but I never really understood it. She said when God asked him what he wanted, his request was wisdom and discernment. In turn, God gave him wisdom and so many other things he didn't ask for, including wealth and nations in which for him to reign. He became one of the greatest kings, all because he asked for wisdom.

After hearing that story as a child, I thought I should ask for wisdom so I could receive all of the above. (You can see where my heart was at that time. Don't worry; I only did it a couple of times.) It wasn't until way later I finally understood why Solomon asked for wisdom.

We need to be the same way. There's so much to learn and not enough time. My wife and I get so excited talking about what we learn each day. I once saw an interview with Bill Gates, and they asked him what his superpower would be if he could have one. He said he wanted to be able to read faster. To many, that wouldn't seem great. Most of us would wish to be able to fly or have super strength. Without sounding too cliché, "Knowledge is power." Bill Gates understands that, and so should we. Just remember, it's *applied* knowledge that is power!

It's estimated that the average millionaire reads three to five books a month. Some of us don't even read two books a year! Then, we wonder why we can't get out of certain situations. My life started to take a huge turn once I started to read more. Our mind starts to expand, new ideas form, and our mindset skyrockets to higher thinking.

The Social Science Research journal found that children raised in a home where there is a library of eighty books

> Formal education will make you a living; self-education will make you a fortune.
> —Jim Rohn

or more have higher literacy levels.[6] According to the study, being surrounded by a lot of books at home help children build vocabulary, increase awareness and comprehension, and expand horizons, which benefits them in adulthood. Simply put, a book-filled home encourages a culture of reading for enjoyment and discussion. Kids will see the joy of reading instead of dreading it as can happen in school.

Proverbs 3:14-17 tells us, "Wisdom is worth more than silver; it brings more profit than gold. Wisdom is more precious than rubies; nothing you could want is equal to it. With her right-hand wisdom offers you a long life, and with her left hand, she gives you riches and honor. Wisdom will make your life pleasant and will bring you peace."

We tend to undervalue how important it is to continue learning. Countless times, I've heard people say they are excited to get out of high school or college because they no longer have to learn anything. This type of thinking is a real shame. Learning doesn't stop when we walk out of school; that's when it begins. The old saying, "You learn something new every day," should be our goal. On several occasions, Warren Buffet said we should go to bed smarter than how we woke up.

Think about it. If we learn one tiny fact every day and try to improve 1% daily, how will we be at the end of a year? We would know 365 facts and be 365% better every year! It doesn't take much. Go to the closest public library or bookstore and look through the non-fiction section. See what topics interest you that you can start learning.

As Proverbs 2:2 advises us, "Turn your ears to wisdom, and concentrate on understanding." We'll cover more about wisdom in later chapters when we start talking about investing. I wanted to plant the seed that learning is essential for our future. In the next chapter, we'll learn why it's so essential.

Action Step 4

We must always be growing and learning. I feel overwhelmed by how much there is to learn, and it feels like I don't have enough time or that I am not learning fast enough. Take the time to write down at least five things that you would like to learn. They don't have to be extravagant, just something you would like to develop a skill in and then focus on each one, one at a time. All it takes is to set aside some time each day to learn something about it. Even if you only have fifteen minutes, eventually the skill will begin to take shape.

_____

_____

_____

_____

_____

_____

_____

CHAPTER 9

SHEEP AMID WOLVES

And you shall know the truth,
and the truth shall set you free.

—John 8:32

Ignorance isn't bliss. If we want to be better at something, we have to know what that something is and learn how to get better. And to be financially free, we need to know the truth about finances.

In this section so far, we covered shifting our mindset to know we live in a world of abundance. We also now know knowledge is more valuable than anything else.

We don't have to be born into wealth or suddenly get an unimaginable raise at our job. All we have to know is how it all works. We have to understand there are certain principles we can follow to be financially free. We aren't financially free, and we're in debt because we don't know the principles! It's okay; I'm going to give the necessary knowledge to be able to bless our families and be able to leave an inheritance to our children.

This book will tell the truth about money and how to use it for its intended purpose.

Most of us think that we have to be lucky or deceiving to have more money. The truth is, all we need to know is how money works. Once we understand how it works, then we can start making it work for us.

It's going to take some time to get there, but hard things are worth it until it becomes natural. This is our first stepping stone to getting the knowledge we need to start making a difference in our lives.

Losing Weight and Building Wealth

Probably two of the most common things we want are obtained in much the same way on a macro level, even though they seem to be two different things.

When I was about twenty-two years old, I was extremely overweight, especially for my size. I'm a short guy, and weighing 210lbs didn't help. In high school, I barely tipped the scale at 120lbs. In three years, I gained ninety lbs. I worked at a desk fixing computers, and people fed me, hoping I'd make quick repairs.

I realized I gained weight and had to lose it. It's much easier to gain weight than to lose weight. I didn't know the first thing to do. Sure, everyone says work out and eat right—that's the secret! It's a lot like me saying, "Just save and invest in building wealth. That's the secret!"

I tried eating right and started working out, but the scale wouldn't move more than five pounds after trying for what felt like forever. I tried everything from fad diets to starving myself (I didn't last long doing that one). I went to the gym, and I had no idea what I was doing. I even started running, but still, nothing seemed to work.

After six years of trying, I only was able to lose twenty pounds. I was twenty-eight and 190 pounds. I was fed up! I didn't like how I felt, and I hated dressing up nicely because I was uncomfortable in everything. I was done!

Then, without realizing it, I started to read more about weight loss. I applied different principles that worked for other people. I went to the gym and tried the workouts (I still felt awkward). I bought anything equated to working out, weight loss, and a six-pack.

I went to Walmart and picked up every magazine, *Men's Health, Fitness, Fitness Rx, Muscle & Fitness, Men's Fitness*. If it had a muscular guy on the cover, I bought it. I read them cover to cover every month. I bought workout books and books about lifting. I even bought a personal training course so I could learn more.

Within a year, I went from 190lbs, 30% body fat, down to 150lbs, 9% body fat.

What was the difference? I gained knowledge and understanding. But let me be clear—knowledge didn't make it any easier. For the first six months, it was beyond painful. But I kept at it. I ate right, went to the gym, and put in my tears and sweat.

It was knowledge, understanding, time, commitment, and persistence that made the difference. Rome wasn't built in a day, and anything worth it is going to take time. But you also have to be willing to take the hits. There were countless times when family members or friends wanted me to eat things I knew weren't going to help my progress.

I heard things like, "Why? Are you on a diet or what? One bite won't hurt. It's a birthday party. It's a holiday. It's Friday." They sure didn't make things easier.

Why am I saying this?

Because the same thing is going to happen when it comes to money. People don't like being told you can't do something because you don't want to stray away from your goals.

I realized one thing after that happened. When I was little, I loved to learn, as I mentioned earlier. But I thought there were only two kinds of books—fiction and textbooks. I didn't like reading fiction, so I read textbooks—primarily science and biology books. I didn't know there were so many other available books for different things.

I didn't know there were books on how to learn about money. I didn't realize it until right after I learned how to lose weight and applied it. That's a critical point; knowledge without action is useless.

As soon as I realized that, guess what I did? I went out and bought books and magazines that had anything to do with money. There are many books I recommend starting with *Rich Dad, Poor Dad*. This one opened my eyes to what was going on in the world when it came to money. I learned we needed to have a financial IQ to be financially free.

We need to know the truth!

Here's the scary part. The government doesn't want our children to know about money; they don't want *us* to know about money. They want us to believe in the American Dream. However, the American dream is not a fairy tale dream for us. It's become a marketing scheme, selling it to us to turn us into assets for the government and the banks. Let's look at it; they tell us to go to college and get a higher education, get one job so you can buy a house, a nice car, get some credit cards, and buy ourselves nice things. In doing those things, we accumulate sources of debt for us like student loans, a mortgage, an auto loan, and some credit card debt.

> Intelligence solves problems and produces money. Money without financial intelligence is money soon gone.
> —Robert Kiyosaki

So, now we have to remain in our *one* job, as an employee, to pay higher taxes than business owners and investors. The American Dream made us into a cash-flowing asset for the government and banks. Is there any wonder why they wouldn't teach us financial literacy?

It is because they make the rules! The good news is that anyone can use these rules; they're basic principles. All we have to do is recognize them.

We all go to schools where they teach us how to stay within the lines, learn a certain way, and not think for ourselves. They want factory workers to make them richer. We live in a society kept in the dark; all we have to do is turn on the light.

These principles are already given to us in the Bible to follow. There are also rules in our society we can follow to build wealth for ourselves, our families, our children, and, most importantly, for God's kingdom. We only need to learn these principles and rules. We are sheep and must go out among the wolves of our government, banks, and institutions and learn to be wise as snakes and work within the law to be as innocent as doves.

The above is the main reason I wrote this book. I want you to know how money works the same way the rich do. I want you to know that knowledge is everywhere, and you can take full advantage of the laws and come out on top.

We weren't given these principles in school, so I want to be sure we're fully equipped. The education system has conditioned us to avoid mistakes and to follow the patterns set before us. We need to learn how to break free from those patterns.

* * *

In the next section, I'll show you exactly what money is and how you can start using it intentionally.

SECTION THREE
WHAT IS MONEY?

If your wealth increases,
don't make it the center of your life.

—Psalms 62:10 NLT

CHAPTER 10
TRUE RICHES

A feast is made for laughter, wine makes life merry, and money is the answer for everything.

—Ecclesiastes 10:19

In this chapter, I'll uncover how important money is and how important it is to learn how to use it.

Money. When we hear that word, it takes our minds to certain places. Nobody likes talking about it; it's rude to ask how much a person makes, and it's not a topic of discussion in the same way politics and religion are taboo subjects, but it's the backbone of our economy. It makes the world work; it helps us live and carries our day-to-day activities. But we can't talk about it?

Parents would rather speak to their kids about sex than about money and investing, and that's primarily because most parents don't know much about money themselves. Where did we go wrong? Why is it rude to ask? Do we ever stop to ask ourselves that? I did! It's because everyone is always trying to be better than the next, and no one wants to feel inferior. You most certainly aren't supposed to ask your coworkers. *Why?* Because our employer is trying to make sure the peace isn't broken. People get paid differently, even if they're in the same position.

The Bible and Jesus Himself spoke more about money than anything else. Sixteen out of the thirty-eight parables talk about money! How much more did He talk about money?

The Bible has 2,350 verses on money. There are just a little over 500 verses in the Bible on prayer, and a little less than 500 verses on faith, but there are 2,350 verses about money.[7]

If it was important to God, shouldn't it also be relevant to us?

There are many warnings about money and what not to do with it. God was obvious in his instructions for worldly wealth.

He says:

- Don't trust it.
- Don't love it.
- Don't lay it up (hoard it) for yourself upon the Earth.

Even with all these warnings, none of them say don't have it. We need money in our lives to be able to provide for our families. 1 Timothy 5:8 says, "Anyone who does not provide for their relatives, and especially for their own household, has denied the faith and is worse than an unbeliever." Money is the reason why we work; it's why we put in the hours. It's necessary to put food on the table and a roof over our heads. This is a direct order! We don't have to be a believer to understand how important it is to provide for our household.

We work; we make money, and yet, we aren't supposed to talk about it? Do we have to see it as evil? We're to believe we need to be poor to seek the kingdom of God? This can't be how it's supposed to be—this is a false doctrine.

We don't have to believe we need to be poor and live paycheck to paycheck. That's not right at all. Besides, when we live paycheck to paycheck, we're living well above our means. I'm not saying we have to be rich; I'm saying we have to be smart with our money. I hear people all the time say we have to be content with what we have. We can't want to make more money. And these are the same people who live paycheck to paycheck with credit card debt and stress. How can we give ourselves to God if we are under constant stress?

As a side note, if we have credit card debt, we aren't content with what we have. We've put stuff on credit we couldn't afford, and it's accumulated into debt—just a little tough love.

It is one thing to live humbly. Warren Buffett has billions of dollars but lives humbly. Another thing is living above our means. And if America's statistics mean anything, 95% of us live above our means.

That alone is a sin in and of itself. After all, how can we help and be kind to the poor if we're living above your means? We must help the poor, and we can't help someone out of a hole if we're standing right next to them.

We'll talk more about this in later chapters, but it stands to reason that when we've piled up debt, we have a white-knuckle grip on money. That's because it's not ours; it's the lenders! So, how are we to help the needy?

Okay, I'm sure most think we can help by giving of our time. I'm all for going and helping out, but let's be realistic. How often are we able to go out of our way and give our time away? When we have a family at home, it can be challenging to give it to someone else.

If we can understand how important money is, then we can use it to help more people. When we use time and money together, we can cover more ground.

* * *

Matthew 20:26 (NKJV) says, "Yet it shall not be so among you; but whoever desires to become great among you, let him be your servant." We need to serve others. We now understand how vital money is to us and for our economy. But it wasn't always like this. In the next chapter, we'll see where it all started and how it comes together.

CHAPTER 11

TRUST IN MERE HUMANS

Have I put my trust in money or felt
secure because of my gold?

—Job 31:24 NLT

What Is Money?

First of all, not even the government can define money, and the Google definition doesn't help. It describes it as a *current medium* of exchange.

What we do know is that we use it as an exchange, value for value. We also know that we have four different kinds of money, commodity, receipt, fiat, and fractional.

Commodity money is the most basic of types and one of the earlier ones in use. It worked alongside the bartering system, and it was any item that had value and could be exchanged for a good. Some of the most common types of commodities were anything with intrinsic value, such as precious metals, stones, shells, and yes, gold and silver. When people purchased goods, they trust the value of the purchase and the commodity.

Receipt money was the first paper money. This was a receipt of value, depending on how much commodity value you had. If a person had too many silver or gold coins to carry around, they would give them to a goldsmith, who already had protection and vaults to store valuables. In turn, the goldsmith would provide them with a receipt for the value of the deposit minus a fee. These receipts would have "PAY TO THE BEARER ON DEMAND." People would know that it was backed by something of value.

Then, we have the fiat money as we know it today, paper money that is a legal tender and does not have anything of intrinsic value. The term legal tender means that there is a law requiring everyone to accept it as currency. Paperbacked by faith.

Today, money is a question of confidence. Currency today isn't money; the only reason it has any purchasing power whatsoever is that yesterday it purchased something. Hence, you have faith that it is going to buy something tomorrow. Our faith is the only thing carrying the value.

Lastly, we have fractional or commercial bank money because banks typically use this type of money in banknotes and loans, which is a loan given that is worth more than the actual currency they hold, part receipt, and part fiat. For example, Peter provides a goldsmith or bank a thousand dollars' worth of gold, and Peter gets a receipt for that deposit. The goldsmith or bank uses that gold as a backing for lending Paul, Mark, John, and Matthew each a thousand. The gold backs only a thousand, but each borrower only gets a fraction of it supported by the gold. By the way, banks do this *all the time*.

Interestingly enough, as the fraction of receipt money becomes smaller, it slowly starts to transition from fractional to fiat money until there is no more of the fraction and becomes 100% fiat. And here we are.

Where Did Money First Start?

Anyone would say the first currency began with bartering. And for the most part, it makes sense. But it's not entirely true.

Back in the beginning, they didn't have the paper money we have now, but they did need a medium of exchange. Bartering isn't a perfect system, and it can become very inefficient very fast.

We'd have to keep track of each item and what we considered equivalent to those items to trade with something else. Now, let's say we wanted bread, but we only had eggs. We'd need to find someone with bread who wanted eggs at the same time you needed the bread. That would be a coincidence of wants. It's easily maintained if we were working with one single item.

But what if we needed milk and different types of vegetables? That coincidence of wants would be a little harder to time. As indicated in *The Background of Economics* by Merlin Hunter and Gordon Watkins, it's next to impossible for all wishes of bartering individuals to coincide as each person places different value to the kind, quality, and quantity of things mutually desired.

This is one of the things wrong with bartering in any civilized society. There had to have been a mutually understood method of exchange. So, of course, we'd think of silver and gold. However, thousands of years before the invention of coinage, there were interest-bearing loans in Mesopotamia. Which indicates that debt was the forerunner of money.[8]

Not a lot has changed since then. As David Icke puts it, "Money doesn't exist it's only a theory." We give power to the value of the dollar. "Federal Reserve Note" on our dollar indicates it's a note or loan from the Federal Reserve. They're simply obligations to the government, and our debt and faith in it only back it.

A dollar bill is a note of debt. Our entire money supply is backed by nothing but more debt. The 1941 Governor of the Federal Reserve System, Marriner Eccles, stated "That is what our money system is. If there were no debts in our money system, there wouldn't be any money."

> The pieces of green paper have value because everybody thinks they have value.
> —Milton Friedman

Robert Hemphill, a previous Credit Manager of the Federal Reserve Bank in Atlanta, was also quoted saying "If all the bank loans were paid, then no one could have a bank deposit, and there would not be a dollar of coin or currency in circulation." This means that if everyone paid off all of their debt, there would be no money in circulation. How crazy is that?!

Our entire economic standing is a debt based on the faith we give the paper notes. And according to the Bureau of Labor Statistics, there has been a ninety percent decline in purchasing power of the dollar since 1971.

What else happened in 1971? Richard Nixon removed the dollar from the gold standard. Before that, our bills were marked "Certificate" and "Payable to the bearer on demand." Now, it says "This note is legal tender for all debts." That note means our money is no longer backed by gold, and the reserve can print money out of thin air. Mayer Amschel Rothschild says, "Give me control of a nation's money supply, and I care not who makes its laws."

And that is precisely what they did. But as more money is printed, inflation happens, which affects us all. That ninety percent loss of purchasing power is quietly transferred to the federal government in the form of hidden taxation—the Federal Reserve System was how it was accomplished.[9] So, how do they do this?

When money is printed, it becomes fiat and gives the government instant purchasing power without taxation. Since fiat money doesn't have anything to back it, it needs to get money from somewhere like gold. So, it is collected from our purchasing power in the same way a tax is, but unbeknownst to us.

This can be one long and exhausting chapter on how the Federal Reserve started back in 1913 and how they can manipulate the economy by bailouts and printing money. That isn't the point of this book. I merely wanted to shine a little bit of light into how money began and how it is now.

But the future looks mighty interesting. According to investing.com, the current list says there are 1,658 cryptocurrencies. Most of us have only heard of Bitcoin, so this might have blown our minds. Nowadays, most of us don't carry cash around. We have it all on our debit cards and even on our phones. We're coming to an electronic world, and it's coming fast.

In simple terms, cryptocurrency is a digital type of currency with encryption—it's virtual money proven to be more secure and unlike the centralized dollar, meaning it goes through a bank and is controlled from consumer to receiver. Cryptocurrency goes from the consumer straight to the receiver.

I suggest picking up a book on cryptocurrencies. I recommend *Cryptoassets: The Innovative Investor's Guide to Bitcoin and Beyond*. The link will be in recommended book section in the back of this book.

It's been a long road for money, but we can surely know it was created with intention. In the following chapter, I'll go over scripture that shows us exactly what that intention is.

CHAPTER 12
AND IT WAS GOOD

*For everything God created is good, and
nothing is to be rejected if it is received
with thanksgiving.*

—1 Timothy 4:4

How do we know money is good? How do we know
we must understand how to use it wisely and that
it's for us? Well, because it's in scriptures.

In this chapter, I'll show where money started, who
it's for, and for what.

God has a design for everything; there's a principle
set in place for everything He created. That includes all
people, plants, and the smallest bacteria. Everything He
creates has a design to it. This is true even if we may
not see it or science can't explain it.

I was watching a documentary on the universe, and
physicists and astrologers tried to discover the secrets
of the universe. In the end, they all agree on one thing.
They don't know how it was created, but it works for
our benefit. Who would have thunk it?

Luckily for us, we're not talking about the universe but something that's within our grasp every single
day. And the answers have already been given to us in
scripture.

God's original design for wealth and money follow
three simple principles:

1. Providence
2. Possession
3. Provision

Let's go one by one and see how this all relates to us.

A Providence

Providence—God put it there for us to find. He provided it in advance. The first thing we know about money is it wasn't the way we use and see it today. When we think of money, we see a nice crisp, green paper bill. But before it was foldable for a quick slip in our pocket, it was in the form of gold.

Let's go back to the beginning of time. After God created Adam right before Eve, God mentions four headwaters in the Garden of Eden. One of those lands was called Havialah. And in that land, there was gold.

As we mentioned in the previous chapter, before Nixon was president, money was backed by gold. Gold has always been a type of currency; in our case, it's money.

To add some perspective, in the book of Genesis, we see that God made everything, and He said it was good every time he made something. He made the waters, and they were good. He made the plants, and they were good, etc. Then, he put the gold there. He said gold was good in Genesis 2:11-12 (NKJV) "Where there is gold, and the gold of that land is good." How do we know that gold is good? Because God said it was good. And gold was used as one of the first currencies.

So, we can't say money is evil when God himself said, "There is gold, and the gold of that land is good."

The funny thing about gold is that there seems to be a debate on why it's the chosen standard and why we see this metal as precious. Even today, when money isn't defined, we know that gold is the "Gold Standard." But why has it been chosen as the universal money?

There seems to be just the right amount for it to keep its value, but there isn't as much as there is silver, but it's more than there is platinum. Both standards of which are also used and are valuable metals. Gold, however, is where the porridge is just right.

Why? Because God put it there and said it was good. But why in the Garden of Eden? There are no stores, and only two people would inhabit that land.

Because He was providing it for us in advance to be used by us, remember, God doesn't make anything by mistake.

A Possession

Possession—designed it for us to have, the state of having, owning, or controlling something.

So, we know that God placed gold as providence, and we know that it was good. Then, it doesn't mention gold again until he describes it further. It was a possession for his people to have. A requirement as one of the things that made a person wealthy.

Abram had become very wealthy in livestock and in silver and gold. Genesis 13:2 tells us that when God blessed Abram (Abraham), he was blessed to be the first man to be rich in the Bible. He had land, cattle, and of course, gold. Let's not forget that Abram was extremely obedient to God's commands and would drop anything that God asked of him. He left his town and was about to sacrifice his son. His obedience was the reason why the Lord blessed him.

Now, we know that gold (currency/money) was placed here and for our possession. It is ours to use and to have. But there is one more reason why God made gold.

A Provision

Provision—The action of providing or supplying something for use. We use it as an exchange of value, and the value of gold is meant to come to us through other people, as we see in Genesis 41:42. "Then Pharaoh took his gold ring from his finger and put it on Joseph's finger. He dressed him in robes of fine linen and put a gold chain around his neck."

I wanted to make something abundantly clear. When I say "to us," I mean God's people. As believers, we are God's children, and all his creation is for us. The principles, design, and structure are for us to learn and use. We need to know the manner in which he intended for us to use his creation.

Now that you know money was created for us to use and have, we'll now find out one of the main reasons we need to have it. In the next chapter, we'll go over exactly why God wants to bless us.

CHAPTER 13
BLESSED ARE THE MEEK

If you ignore criticism, you will end in poverty and disgrace; if you accept correction, you will be honored.

—Proverbs 13:18 NLT

By now, we know money is for us to use. However, we should understand how to use it and how to obtain it. Remember, there are many warnings about money in the Bible and Jesus' teachings, so we must use it wisely.

We're told not to trust it, love it, or hoard it, but we're never told not to have it. On the contrary, we need to be wise with it.

Before we get into that, let's take a look at the good, the bad, and the ugly side of money. We need to realize how it affects and shapes our lives. If we don't know the truth about something, how can we expect to be free from it?

The Good

Ephesians 4:28 (NLT) tells us, "… use your hands for good hard work, and then give generously to others in need." Besides all things, money is one of the most excellent tools. It's not something we should squander away, work for, pay the bills, and be done. When putting it into the proper hands, money can do many great things.

The lack of money is the root of all evil.
—Mark Twain

As we use a hammer to build and create new things, we can also use that hammer to destroy and break. The same goes for money. We can use it to build, create, and help.

It's by far one of the greatest tools we can use to help our family and our community.

We're to work, and with that work, we're to bring in an income to which we can provide for others. We can't neglect that duty given to us. A lot of us are concerned about ourselves, but the world is much greater than us.

The difference we can make in someone's life can be extraordinary. We need to ask to be blessed so we can be a blessing. Now, this is only a fraction of what we can do but giving generously has many benefits. It sets us up to have an *abundance mentality*. Giving loosens the tight knuckle grasp we grew up with. Remember, we can't expect to receive a dollar when we have a tight fist around a penny.

Let me take a moment here and say our whole purpose of giving shouldn't be to receive. Our heart has to be in the right place. I know in our nature, we always tend to think, *What's in it for me?* But we need to look past that. Giving with an open heart is the real blessing.

When we generously give, we extend the kingdom of God. When we give to someone in need out of the kindness of our heart, we show them God is answering their prayers. Someone is providing for them. It extends thanksgiving both ways—we'll be thankful we have enough to give, and they'll be grateful for the gift. This is the meaning of when they say it's better to give than to receive. We're allowed to have leftovers so we can be a blessing to someone else.

Psalm 112:5-7 (NLT) tells us, "Good comes to those who lend money generously and conduct their business fairly. Such people will not be overcome by evil. Those who are righteous will be long remembered. They do not fear bad news; they confidently trust the LORD to care for them."

The Bad

Ecclesiastes 5:10 (NLT) says, "Those who love money will never have enough. How meaningless to think that wealth brings true happiness!"

In this world, where there's good, there's also bad. We all know and have heard about the wrong money can do and the greed and love that come with it. This is the reason why Jesus preached so much about it. It's a slippery slope when we have a lot of money. We think the more we have, the happier we'll be. We put our complete faith in money and what it can do for us.

We fail to realize God has given it to us. He can take it away in an instant, and then what? We fall back to relying on him. But why must we have everything worldly taken away from us to remember that God is our true source? We talked about this already, but it bears repeating because we're stubborn. Look at the Israelites. God had to keep them in the desert for forty years to show them who was in control. And even then, they still disobeyed and created idols.

How much better are we?

The Ugly

Luke 12:15 (NLT) reminds us to "Beware! Guard against every kind of greed. Life is not measured by how much you own."

The ugly part of money is the first thing we think of when we talk about money are the wealthy. The wealthy are the ones our mother warned us about. They're greedy, deceiving rich people who don't care about anyone or anything other than money. And Mom wasn't wrong.

Banks, financial institutions, the federal reserve, and the entire economy is controlled by the ultra-rich. They created a system that only benefits them and their pockets, which is why I wrote this book—the wealthy created rules and regulations. And the more people kept in the dark, the better for them.

We have been accustomed to taking it as is without question. We go to a bank and get a loan for our benefits, and that's where it ends. We don't think that the bank is lending us money that they created by a click of a mouse and then collecting interest on it. As we learned earlier, they are making money off of us by giving us money they created from debt.

Want to know what happens if we default on a loan? For starters, it costs them next to nothing, but they can't write off the bad loans, so they take the loan and roll it over and increase the amount. Doing this increases the interest amount, it gives the borrower more money to spend, and they can continue paying the interest. Win-win, right?

We operate in a system designed to keep most people from achieving financial freedom. Since the 1800s, we were another cog in the machine, and we were trained to be factory workers who paid taxes. However, it's not the government's fault; it's our own. We need to learn how the system works so we can work within it.

We live in a fallen world with corruption running rampant. This world belongs to the enemy. This is his kingdom, and he'll do what he can to prevent us from taking it back. This is why there are so many wealthy, evil people, and this is also the reason why we, as Christ followers, need to educate ourselves on money. The enemy wants us to think money is evil and that it is wrong to want. He understands it was meant for us to do good in the world.

> For wisdom is protection just as money is protection, But the advantage of knowledge is that wisdom preserves the lives of its possessors.
> -Ecclesiastes 7:12

Before we continue, I want to make the point that this is Satan's Kingdom and why we are instructed to not be of the world. This is the reason so many bad things happen. The truth is that we are the ones that handed it over to him. Remember in Genesis? We were given dominion, but that dominion was given to the serpent when Adam and Eve ate from the forbidden tree.

In Matthew 4:8-9, Satan attempts to tempt Jesus; the devil took him up to a very high mountain, and he showed him all the kingdoms of the world in their magnificence and said to Him, "All these I shall give to you if you will bow down and worship me."

If they weren't his, Jesus would have corrected him, but instead, he just replied, "Away from me, Satan! For it is written: 'Worship the Lord your God, and serve him only.'"

This is why we need to be more vigilant. We need to learn the truth so that we can will not be destroyed for our lack of knowledge as it is written in Hosea 4:6.

* * *

In the next chapter, I'll show how the poor, middle class, and the rich use their money. The best part of it is we can start using our money like the rich right away. The process and principles are the same for everyone. I'll show you what you should have learned in school.

CHAPTER 14
WALK WITH THE WISE

Take a lesson from the ants, you lazybones.
Learn from their ways and become wise!

—Proverbs 6:6 NLT

How do we start living better and creating a better future? The answer is simple. Find out what the wealthy are doing and do the same. Financially free people are no different than anyone else. The only difference is they found out how money works for them.

Yes, it's that simple. All we have to do is find out what is working for them and do the same.

In this chapter, I'll show how the poor use their money, so we don't do that. I'll also show how the rich use their money so we can start implementing it right away. It's all about setting up the proper foundation. Let's get started!

Proverbs 13:20 tells us, "Walk with the wise and become wise."

The problem is they live differently than the rest of the world. We pay far more attention to the way everyone else lives, and we fall into the trap. It's hard to start living differently because everyone around us has influenced us. Our government has programmed us to live that type of life. And we don't even realize it.

We need to break away and learn how to work the system. And the first step in doing so is finding out what everyone else is doing, and do the opposite.

Does that seem odd? Well, it should. Think about it for a second. Here are some statistics to help.

According to insurance industry statistics, out of 100 people working from ages twenty-five to sixty-five (forty-five years),

- One becomes rich
- Four become financially independent
- Five are still working
- Twenty-eight are dead
- Sixty-two are broke

In a nutshell, 5% make it financially, and 95% don't. Is there any wonder why we see people past sixty-five years of age working the door at Walmart?

Now, we know those statistics, so let's ask ourselves if we want to live like the 95%, or do we want to live like the 5%? This isn't about being rich. It's about being in a place of freedom. Living paycheck to paycheck even with a degree isn't freedom. No matter how much we make, we can spend it all and live paycheck to paycheck.

"7 out of 10 college students stress about money."[10] According to a new survey by Ramsey Solutions, money fights are the second leading cause of divorce behind infidelity. Those numbers are staggering. I, for one, don't want to live like the majority of people. But what are we to do? The first thing we're going to do is find out how the majority lives, so we know what *not* to do. Then, we're going to learn how the rich live, so we know what *to* do.

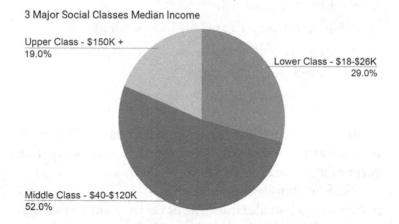

3 Major Social Classes Median Income

Upper Class - $150K +
19.0%

Lower Class - $18-$26K
29.0%

Middle Class - $40-$120K
52.0%

Median household income by income tier in
U.S. states and the District of Columbia, 2016.[11]

As you can see, being in the upper class doesn't mean
we're financially and stress-free. It's not the amount
of money we make; it's how we use it. We can make
$250,000, but if we spend it trying to keep up with the
Joneses, then we're living paycheck to paycheck, not
financially free, and in constant stress about money,
this would be considered high income poor. In the same
respect, even if we're labeled in the poverty class, we
can still be financially free.

The chart above illustrates the social classes we have
here in the U.S. But it doesn't show how each class uses
their money. Let's forget how we're classified, and start
focusing on how there are levels and how each level
utilizes their income.

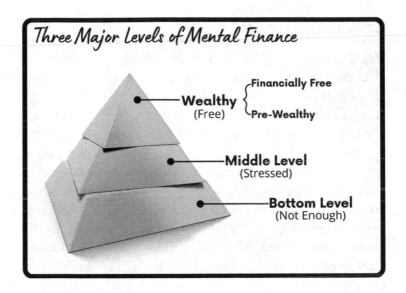

Three Major Levels of Mental Finance

There are three types of levels when it comes to mental finance:

1. Bottom Level: The Poor—Not enough
2. Middle Level: Stressed
3. Top Level: Wealthy—Free

    o   Pre-Wealthy
    o   Financially Free

I want us to start thinking and acting like the wealthy, but before we do, let's look at how each level (bottom, middle, and top) works and, most importantly, how the majority does so we can do the opposite. Let's start with the lower of the bunch.

Bottom Level: The Poor

For the most part, the people in poverty are the group that can't get out of where they are. They live paycheck to paycheck, and their primary concern is to pay the bills. Their entire life is to work and pay bills, and they never seem to have enough. Their system is getting money with time put in usually a 9-5. It's not easy. I grew up in this level, and for the longest time, I was a part of it—the majority of my life was in a poor state. My parents didn't know any other way, and in turn, this was modeled for me. When I grew up, I was still in the same state of mind. Most of us know how it works and have probably been there before, and some might even be there now.

The money of the poor works in this manner.

It's as simple as it looks. We have a job that provides our income. With this income, our only goal is to pay the bills. Everything we make is spent on our monthly requirements. We end up with $0 at the end of the month, and we have no room for anything else. We can make $10,000 or $100,000, but if the cost of all our expenses equals what we bring in, then we're in the poor state category. I can't stress this enough. At the end of the month, we end up with nothing and one to three paychecks away from catastrophe. We need to keep working to pay the bills to keep on living.

The Middle Level: Stressed

The middle level is where the majority in the U.S. live. We have a good-paying job but still feel the tight squeeze due to bills and debt. Most of this group has accrued student debt and several credit cards while trying to keep up with the Joneses.

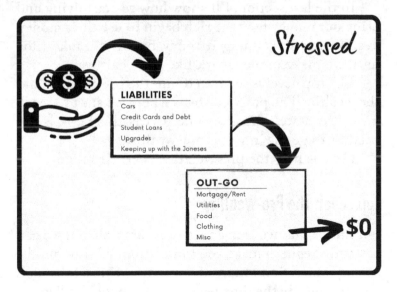

Most of the people in this level operate with a scarcity mentality and want more. The income is much higher, but with every raise, it's time for an upgrade. They get a higher paying job, but then it's time for a new car. They get an increase, but before that first paycheck, they put stuff on a credit card. They'll be able to pay the monthly payment, after all. This group also has the unused gym memberships, extra package channels for the TV, and other memberships that add up.

If this sounds all too familiar, don't worry, a lot of us are there. The difference is now we know. And it's just like everything; the first step is accepting and knowing the difference. This middle level has a nasty habit of getting deeper and deeper into debt. It usually starts with a student loan, then a car, then a house, then credit cards. The middle class's currency is debt, and everything coming in goes to it, including the mortgage. Yes, a house is a liability, *not* an asset. We'll go more in detail about that later in an upcoming chapter.

In the last section, I'll show how to start living and using our money how the rich begin to use their money. Yes, we can start doing it today, but it will take time until we make money work like the wealthy.

The top-level is separated into the pre-wealthy and the wealthy. The pre-wealthy is where we start to reach a wealthy state. The awesome part is this book is the catalyst to get us into the pre-wealthy.

Here is how the pre-wealthy use their money.

Top Level: The Pre-Wealthy

For most of us, we aren't going to start rich, but we can certainly begin to make the foundation. We can build a strong foundation today, so our house will last through generations. By the time we finish this book, we'll know exactly how to become pre-wealthy. Unlike the bottom level we will learn to buy time with money, giving us more time and ultimately more money.

Before we get into it, I also want us to understand the huge difference between being rich and being wealthy. A rich person can have a job and make a million dollars but gets taxed 37% and keeps a little over half. A wealthy person collects assets, accumulating an income of a million dollars, gets taxed about 20%, and keeps well over half.

The wealthy understand it's not how much money we make; it's how much we get to keep. Here's the fine print. To have a wealthy life, we'll need to sacrifice today. As we discussed losing weight, there are certain things we'll need to learn and things we'll need to put aside or remove from our life. We have to be willing to live a few years like most people won't, so we can spend the rest of our life like most people can't.

Here is the foundation on how to do so.

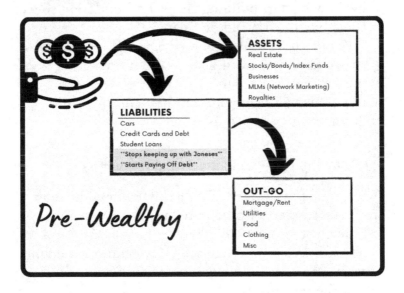

Most of our current income will go to multiple assets. We'll go over them in the next chapters. There's no need to worry if we don't know about some of them. For now, I want us to understand what we need to start doing and how we can do the opposite of what 95% of people are doing so we can live like the 5%.

If we're thinking we don't have the money to start putting it into assets, that's okay. The income is going out to liabilities, and we need to start paying off all debt and removing unnecessary things. The sad part is that most people know that they need to start tithing, saving and investing. However, the problem is that after they pay for all of their liabilities and expenses, they have no money to do any of the rest. Ultimately making tithing, saving, and investing the last priority if at all.

Yup, sorry, that monthly gym membership we never use has to go. As I stated earlier, we'll be discussing this stage in great detail. By the end of this book, we'll know how to start building this very foundation so we can live like the 5% and be financially free.

It's not going to happen overnight. If we start with what we have and learn how to use money instead of money using us, we can provide a better life for our family. This will teach our children and our children's child the proper way to use money.

The Very Top Level: Wealthy—Financially Free

After some time, there will be a shift in how the money we invested starts working for us. As my uncle says, "Money just sitting in the bank is lazy money, and we don't want to have lazy money." If we commit a couple of years of life to set a correct foundation, we'll start seeing the rewards.

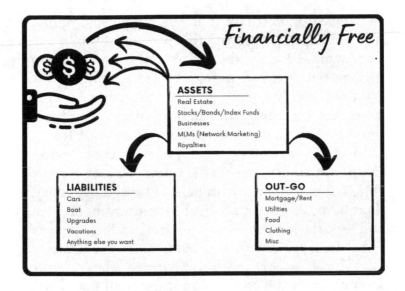

Here is where things begin to look attractive. During that time of sweat, the sacrifice we put in will start to pay us. That's when our money starts *making* us money. Now that our assets start paying us, we can use that to upgrade. We no longer have to worry about having enough income to supply our needs. Our assets begin to pay for everything.

That is the definition of being financially free—when we have our investments and assets pay for our living expenses. At that point, we no longer have to depend on a job or employer. In a sense, we can retire.

We need to get another asset to pay for that upgrade if we decide we want to upgrade. Robert Kiyosaki put it best. When he wanted to purchase a Porsche, he bought an asset that provided the Porsche's monthly cost. Once he got rid of the car, he continued to have the asset still provide the income.

I understand we won't be able to do this right away; if we could, I would already have a couple of Porsches.

What we can do is take it as an example and think of how we can start applying this principle for ourselves. For example, I make the income, so I set a budget to give my wife some spending cash for herself. But then I started to think about Robert's asset to pay for his wants, and I set her up with an investment account under her Ally bank and deposited a set amount. With that money, I invest it in large-company stocks and transfer the profits to her checking account. This does several things, it provides her with personal spending money, I don't have to set aside a budget for extra spending, and I still have the initial deposit amount. Yes, there are risks, but there is no investment that is 100% guaranteed.

We will go over stock investing in a later chapter, so don't worry if it sounds confusing right now. I want you to understand that is that there is a way that we can eventually have our assets pay for the things we need and untimely also the things we want by reinvesting into assets and building wealth. That is true financial freedom.

It will take some work and some diligence on our part. The good news is it's possible. I thought we had to be born rich to be wealthy. But now, I understand it is possible if we follow the principles I outline in this book.

Cash Flow Is King

Cash Flow

The first thing we need to do is understand *Cash Flow*, and it is all dependent on your income and expenses. We will always have expenses such as light, gas, and any utilities needed to sustain our lives. It's the first half of our financial statement. Lucky for us, the math is super simple.

Cash Flow = Income - Expenses

It is composed of two simple parts, everything that is incoming and everything that is outgoing—what you make at your job and the things you pay for monthly. Simple as that.

Balance Sheet

The second half of our financial statement is the balance sheet. It also has two columns, the asset and liability columns. The asset column is everything you own and their value and cash you have available whether in a checking, savings, investment account, while the liability is a list of everything you owe and to whom. This is all loans (personal student, auto) and debt along with your mortgage. The difference between them is your equity or net worth.

Equity (Net Worth) = Assets - Liabilities

So, now, we have six numbers that will give us our overall financial status.

1. Income
2. Expenses
3. Cash flow
4. Assets
5. Liabilities
6. Equity (Net Worth)

We are going to need to focus our attention on cash flow, because as stated, cash flow is king. When we make more than what we spend, we have positive cash flow. However, let's say we borrowed from a bank to purchase a car. That gets listed under liabilities as a promise to pay. As we saw in our middle level, when you have liabilities, they become expenses. If something were to happen to our income, we will be negative cash flow very quickly.

Therefore, it is important to understand where you stand financially and how secure your financial statement is. By taking these numbers down, we can see if your equity is negative because you have more liabilities, or if you have enough cash flow to cover you in the case of hardships and know what areas to improve. The overall goal is to limit your liabilities and increase your assets.

I get super excited talking about this because anyone can do it. These principles have been set in place, so if we start applying them, we too can live a wealthy life. As you can see, all we have to do is start thinking like the rich and treat our money in the same manner. The most significant part of all this is the Bible shows us how to do this. We'll be going over the entire process, and I'll be showing you with Biblical scripture how to accomplish this in further chapters.

We now have a bird's eye on how the rich use their money, so they can eventually have their money work for them. In the following section, I will show exactly how to start doing this, no matter where we're starting from. It's time to level up!

Action Step 5

Calculate your Cash Flow and Equity (Net Worth)!

See where you stand by calculating your cash flow and net worth. You can use the table at the end of this book to write down all of your amounts or download the excel file that will auto calculate for you. Link is in Appendix 2

CASH FLOW

Income - Expenses

EQUITY

Assets - Liabilities

Write Down Your Numbers

Income: _____   Assets: _____

Expenses: _____   Liabilities: _____

Cash Flow: _____   Equity (Net Worth): _____

SECTION FOUR
BEING A GOOD STEWARD

So if you have not been trustworthy with worldly wealth, who will trust you with true riches?

—Luke 16:11

CHAPTER 15
UNDER OUR AUTHORITY

*Moreover, it is required of stewards that
they be found trustworthy.*

—1 Corinthians 4:2 ESVUK

This section will teach us exactly what we need to do to start living a life of wealth. The first thing we need to understand is the level we're at and what we need to do to move up. This is the groundwork for everything this book hopes to accomplish. It's not going to happen overnight, but working at it will increase our financial IQ and, eventually, our bank account.

Stress in the U.S. regarding money is at an all-time high. One out of every three married couples argues about money, making 33% of marriages end in divorce due to financial stress. Worse yet, 72% of Americans have reported feeling stressed about money.[12] I know I've been in that statistic several times in my life. The numbers don't stop there. 76% of American households live paycheck to paycheck.[13] It's no wonder the loss of a job causes 35% of homelessness.[14]

The main question here is, why? Why are more than half of Americans worried and stressed about money? The problem is we're not in control of the money. Instead, we're letting money and outside forces control us. We give money way too much power and fail to realize we need to direct it. We listen to what marketing and advertising tell us we need to make our lives better. We're broke and stressed about money because we fail to do the one thing required to live financially free. We don't live below our means.

That sentence makes me cringe. But we have to understand there are sacrifices we have to make in the beginning. I'm not asking we live frugal until the day we die. All we have to do is sacrifice a couple of years so we can live better and stress-free later. I keep coming back to losing weight because we all know the secret to lose weight. It's simple—control our eating and exercise. The same goes for becoming financially free—control our money and invest.

So many of us want a better house, a better car, more shoes (sorry ladies), and that's all fine and dandy, but living paycheck to paycheck while racking up debt on credit cards isn't the answer. Listen to me very carefully. The last thing we need is an upgrade. We need a downgrade in the things we don't need so that we can enjoy the things we do.

What Is a Good Steward?

All of this unhappiness, stress, and suffering is rooted in poor stewardship, and it starts because we fail to realize it all belongs to God. God wants to bless us; that's what He does as a Father. But just like a father won't bless his child with ice cream when he's misbehaving, we can't be blessed when we're not in alignment with His teachings.

Robert Morris has preached that, God is good and can't bless a bad steward. His goodness and love prevent it. A steward is entrusted with protecting, maintaining, nurturing, and/or growing things (a business, a farm, a household, or some funds) that belong to someone else.[15] How we handle these things which have been entrusted to us qualifies us for blessings, which we learn in Luke 16:10-11 (NLT), "If you are faithful in little things, you will be faithful in large ones. But if you are dishonest in little things, you won't be honest with greater responsibilities. So, if you have not been trustworthy in handling worldly wealth, who will trust you with true riches?"

Most of the time, I hear people say, "Once I make more money, then I can start saving," or "I don't make enough to make a budget." They fail to realize they don't have enough because they fail to start with what they have. If we can't handle $100, how can we possibly think we'll handle $1,000?

> This is how one should regard us, as servants of Christ and stewards of the mysteries of God.
> —1 Corinthians 4:1 ESV

The concept of this is in the parable of the three servants, which I'll discuss later in this book, but the key point to get from the story is illustrated in two verses in that parable from Matthew 25:15. "To one He gave five bags of gold, to another two bags, and to another one bag, *each according to his ability.*" Then, we learn more in Matthew 25:29 (NLT), "To those who use well what they are given, even more will be given, and they will have an abundance. But from those who do nothing, even what little they have will be taken away."

He gave each of them a bag according to their ability or talent. He will not provide us with more than we are able to be faithful. That would be like giving a ten-year-old a large bag of candies. When God asks us to do something, and we obey, He'll give us more. But if we reject Him and ignore His commands, less will be given to us. It's when we're faithful with Him, His orders, and what He has entrusted us with that He'll bless us with more.

He's given us everything and put it all under our authority to care for it and multiply it. So, how do we begin to be faithful with a little? In this section of the book, we'll go through the principals of becoming good stewards and becoming financially free. But first, we need a plan! As Henry Ford says, "If we fail to plan, we plan to fail."

> You (God) gave them (us) charge of everything you made, putting all things under their (our) authority.
> —Psalms 8:6 NLT

Our end goal is to be financially free, build a wealth foundation for ourselves through investments, and leave an inheritance for our children. So, we know our goals. What we need is a plan.

Here's the basic structure and what we'll be covering in the following chapters:

9 Step Level up Wealth Plan

1. Stop the bleeding and minimize.
2. Tithe.
3. Start an emergency fund with at least $1,000.
4. Command your money.
5. Pay off all debts.
6. Save—Put three to six months of expenses into a money market; this will be your emergency savings.
7. Start investing at least 15% of your income into index funds, Roth IRAs, and pre-tax retirement plans.
8. Give generously.
9. Begin investment funding for your children.

Before we get into the meat of it, let's cover step one here.

What's the first thing we do when someone cuts themselves on something sharp? We stop the bleeding! It's the same thing when it comes to getting our money straight. We need to stop the bleeding. In other words, stop using credit cards and stop all monthly payments we don't need. We need to make a list of all our expenses and start removing everything unimportant. For most of us, this includes gym memberships we don't use. But don't make this an excuse not to stay healthy. If we haven't used it in over a month, cancel it. Go running.

Other miscellaneous bills might include cable TV (I had to cancel this one), satellite TV, the top tier Internet, Netflix, Disney +, and all those other TV subscriptions. If we're not making enough income, the last thing we should do is binge on TV. Cut out anything that's subscription-based we don't need. When I first started, the only thing I had as far as subscription was my Internet because I use it for work and Hulu for the kids, and that's because I got it on sale for $0.99 a month. That was it. I was able to cut out everything else and did whatever I could to minimize what I couldn't remove, like the light. I even sold my Harley! All of this ended up saving me an extra $700 a month, which went to paying off debt. That's up to $8,400 toward debt annually.

Was it easy? Nope! It was one of the hardest things to do. But I don't regret it at all. I still get sad about selling my Harley, though. By the third month, we got so used to it, my wife and I didn't miss any of the subscriptions we canceled. We don't even know why we had them in the first place!

Now that we've removed all of the things tying us down, we can start putting that toward the next step in our game plan. To make it easier, remember, it's not forever. We're doing it until we get out of debt. If we have no debt, well, congratulations, we can move on to the next step!

* * *

In the next chapter, I'll discuss the most important thing we need to do right after removing all the unneeded subscriptions and memberships. We can't afford to skip this step!

Action Step 6

Stop the bleeding!

Go through your expenses and cancel all subscriptions you don't need and especially the ones you don't use.

Remember that some things we don't need we just want to have them. You will need to make some sacrifices along the way, but if you cut out things you don't need you can make room for some things you enjoy.

SUBSCRIPTIONS/SERVICES

Gym Membership

Satellite/Cable TV

Streaming Services (Netflix, Hulu, Disney+, etc.)

Magazine Subscriptions

Softwares

Suppliers

Shippers

Extra Phone Charges

I am sure there are a lot more but you get the idea.

CHAPTER 16
BELONGS TO THE LORD

Will a mere mortal rob God? Yet you rob
me. But you ask, 'How are we robbing
you?' "In tithes and offerings."

—Malachi 3:8

Everyone always wants to be blessed with more, but few take this one thing seriously. The tithe is the most, and I do mean *the most* crucial part of this entire process, even before commanding our money.

It's hard to explain how powerful tithing is. Don't trust me on this, but trust the Lord on this one. If we want more, we need to learn how to give more. It's that simple.

As far back as I can remember, I'd skip the tithe, pass the offering plate to the next person, and hope they didn't notice I didn't put anything in or judge me.

It wasn't until I was thirty-six years old that I started tithing. I'd already been working and getting an income for twenty years! Being honest, it wasn't even my idea to start. My wife had to force me to start giving my tithe. At first, nothing happened. No changes. I did notice I was still able to pay my bills and live month-to-month. But then, I started tithing from my heart, and everything started to change.

For the worst.

Until it got better.

It was a rollercoaster I kept riding. To start, I was self-employed, and I found myself with no income. I'd get a small job, and I'd get paid $300, and I'd tithe $30. Would those $30 have helped? Oh, yeah! They really would have.

There's nothing more aggravating than tithing $15 out of $150 and then receiving a bill for $150 and you can't pay it because you are short $15. That happened several times to me.

But I kept on. Slowly, I started realizing I was paying the bills. Nothing was past due or shut off. I continued to have a roof over my head, clothes on my back, gas in the car, and food in my stomach. I wasn't missing anything. All my needs were met!

So, I pressed on and continued to give my tithe; even if I made $10, I tithed $1.

Then, one month, I didn't get any new clients, and I was down to $0.49 in my bank account. It was a lot better than being in the negative like I had been 100s of times before.

Before I finish this story, I have to say a couple of months before that, there was a flood in my area, and the house I was renting was under almost two feet of water. I had all of my family and friends tell me to claim it so I could get something to help me financially. We decided to take the high road and not claim anything since we were renting it and nothing valuable of ours got damaged.

A couple of weeks went by, and we received a knock on the door from FEMA wanting to do an inspection. We told them we were renting and that nothing of ours got damaged, despite everyone telling us to lie so we could get money from them. We didn't have anything to claim. They left, and that was the end of that.

The new month had come by, and all my bills were due, including rent, and I had less than fifty cents to my name. As I was trying to produce income and figure out how we were going to pay rent, my wife asked me if I had closed a client. I told her I had some people in the pipeline, but nothing had come through yet.

As it turns out, there was a deposit in our bank account for the total amount of all our bills plus rent and a little extra for other necessities. I told the FEMA story because that's the only explanation we have. The deposit didn't say where it was from or who deposited it.

It didn't stop there. Right after, I finally received a check from my previous employer I'd been trying to get for the past year. When I thought there was no other way I could possibly get any more money, I was offered a contract to help an agency. This agency would pay me three times more than any other job I'd been at.

I panicked when they told me they no longer needed the extra help, and my contract was done, but I was okay with it. Shortly after that, I started getting my own clients, and it's slowly grown more and more.

God can do a lot more with 90% than you can with 100%.

Who It's For

One thing I want us to understand is the tithe isn't for God; it's for us. God doesn't need our 10%! His roads are paved in gold, which means it's beneath Him. He doesn't need our tiny 10%.

He even tells us in Psalms 50:12, "If I were hungry, I would not tell you, for the world is mine, and all that is in it."

When we tithe, we bless our income. It's for blessing us; it's not to take away from us. It's adding to what we already have.

Proverbs 11:24-25 (NLT) tells us, "Give freely and become more wealthy; be stingy and lose everything. The generous will prosper; those who refresh other will themselves be refreshed."

Elijah and the Widow

This story takes place in the book of Kings, and it was during a horrible drought. During that time, Elijah was a man of God. God sent him away, and during the drought, God fed him and supplied him with water as we learn in 1 Kings 17:6. "The ravens brought him bread and meat in the morning and bread and meat in the evening, and he drank from the brook." After that, in 1 Kings 17:9, He sent Elijah to a widow so that she may feed him. "Go at once to Zarephath in the region of Sidon and stay there. I have directed a widow there to supply you with food."

Now, this widow lived with her son and was on the brink of death due to the drought. She didn't have enough for herself, much less a third person. When Elijah asked her for some water and then boldly told her to get him some bread to eat, 1 Kings 17:12 the widow replied, "I don't have any bread—only a handful of flour in a jar and a little olive oil in a jug. I am gathering a few sticks to take home and make a meal for myself and my son, that we may eat it—and die."

It's a wonder Elijah didn't stop there and back off. But he continued without even batting an eye. 1 Kings 17:13-14 tells us, "Don't be afraid. Go home and do as you have said. But first, make a small loaf of bread for me from what you have and bring it to me, and then make something for yourself and your son. For this is what the Lord, the God of Israel, says: 'The jar of flour will not be used up and the jug of oil will not run dry until the day the Lord sends rain on the land.'"

The widow went and did as Elijah had instructed. And the promise given to her was fulfilled. The jar of flour was not emptied, and the oil never ran dry until the rain came again, which was three *years* later!—not days, not weeks, or even months. At that time, she only had enough to live one more day, but when she gave first of what she had, everything else was blessed longer than expected.

She'd let go and trusted God would provide. 1 Kings 17:17 tells us, "Sometime later, the son of the woman who owned the house became ill. He grew worse and worse and finally stopped breathing."

Elijah carried the boy to an upstairs room and prayed over the child and brought him back to life. Not only was she blessed with enough food for three years, but her son was brought back to life after a sickness. She was blessed and then blessed some more.

Tithing is putting our trust in God and blessing what He's entrusted us with.

So, this story isn't about Elijah being fed by a widow, but it's about a blessed widow who put her trust in God by giving, even though she had little. Elijah wasn't sent to the widow for himself, but he was sent for her. She's the one who needed to be blessed.

When we tithe, it's the same thing. It's not for God, and it's not only for the church, but it's putting our trust in God and blessing what He's entrusted us with.

We shouldn't worry about not having enough for our needs. Luke 12:31 (NLT) tells us, "Seek the Kingdom of God above all else, and live righteously, and He will give you everything you need." God has taken this responsibility for us. He's obligated Himself to provide for our needs. When I started tithing, I didn't have much in the bank, but I never went hungry, cold, or homeless, and I could still drive to work.

Now, let's go one level deeper.

When we give a tithe, it's not the church we touch, but who the church provides. Our tithe goes a lot further than our reach. Somewhere, someone is asking and praying for help for a blessing and a miracle. Your tithe may be the answer to someone else's prayers.

Malachi 3:10 tells us, "Bring the whole tithe into the storehouse, that there may be food in my house. Test me in this," says the Lord Almighty, "and see if I will not throw open the floodgates of heaven and pour out so much blessing that there will not be room enough to store it."

I can't beat this dead horse any more than I already have. The tithe is essential in blessing our current income, blessing others, and growing our wealth. It's a principle set by God.

Most importantly, you don't need to worry about where the money goes, or what they will do with it. We are supposed to obey God in giving. What they do with it is up to them. They will need to answer to God; we did our part in obeying him.

In 2017, Jeff Bezos was the third richest man in the world. After being criticized for his lack of generosity, he gave an estimated $2 billion to support homeless families. That year, Jeff shot past Bill Gates in net worth.

Before that, Bill Gates lost almost half his net worth back in 1999 to 2005. This started his foundations and charity, and he quickly regained his position as the richest man in the world.

We have to do a little research and some comparison charts to see how being generous and giving has a profound effect on receiving. Imagine the impact it'll have when we give out of our hearts without the expectation of receiving. This is a blessing we can't put a price on.

After we get on a steady roll on tithing, I would recommend starting donations to different charities. One of the best ways I have found to start is to give those extra cents or that dollar more at most cashiers when you're at checkout. This is a small step that we can take to go beyond our tithe and really put us in a gracious state of giving.

* * *

Next, I want to talk about the other not so liked word—saving! When I first started, I had a really tough time with this one. I'm sure you're thinking the same thing. *How can I tithe, pay off my debt, and save when I barely make enough?* Don't worry; I'm going to help get us past that stage.

The next chapter will cover how to save, how much to save, where to save your savings, and most importantly, when to stop!

Action Step 7

Let's start tithing!

Start at your local church or any place that feeds you spiritually.

Keep in mind that there is a difference between tithe and charity. Charity is giving, which is also a very good thing to do. Even if you are not part of a church, there are many ministries and organizations are doing great things throughout the world.

You can find many here: ministryvoice.com/most-trusted-nonprofits

You can also look toward causes that you want to help. For me, it's child trafficking and children with cancer.

Here are a couple of resources that use the majority of donations directly to the people in need and where your money is being used wisely.

WHERE I USUALLY GIVE

compassion.com
worldvision.org/sponsor-a-child
pencilsofpromise.org
stjude.org
ourrescue.org

CHAPTER 17
FOOLS SPEND

The wise have wealth and luxury,
but fools spend whatever they get.

—Proverbs 21:20 NLT

I can't tell you how many times I heard, "You should be saving your money." And I never listened. I remember my mom telling me that my uncle would always say, "Save $20 from every one of your paychecks without fail." Well, I never saw my parents do it, so I never did either. Because we all know that it is a lot easier said than done.

When it comes to money, the first thing we hear is to save it, and then we hear about tithing. It's the two things we don't want to hear. A lot like losing weight, the first things we hear are the last we want to hear. "Eat right and exercise." Reading those two might send chills down someone's spine.

But we can't escape it.

It might even seem counterproductive to be told we should give some of our money to the church, but we must also save. Some might even think if we can't even save, how can we tithe?

I've been there. These two principles are essential to becoming financially free. If we're unable to do both, that means we need to cut back on some things, or we're living well above your means, or perhaps both.

Is the rent too high? Then, move to a smaller place.

Are car payments costing too much? Sell them! Yes, even if we're not going to get the value of the car. They're the worst purchases we can make. Stop eating out so much! Get a crockpot, and start eating at home. Stop shopping for clothes every weekend! And we certainly don't need to splurge on a birthday party or presents. There are so many ways we can limit our spending to start saving and start getting out of debt, but we have to start. It took us years to get where we are, so it will take some struggle to get back to zero. Like everything, it's all worth it.

I'm going to say one thing, though. We don't save for the rest of our life. We won't save ourselves to financial freedom. All we're going to save for is three to six months' worth of all of our expenses, and then stop saving.

Let me repeat that.

Save for three to six months' worth of our expenses, and then stop saving! Proverbs even tells us to be like the ant; it stores it's provisions in the summer. Want to take a quick guess how long summer lasts? If you live in a state that actually has all four seasons, summer is three months. The ant doesn't keep saving, and neither should you.

Your First Savings

When we're in debt, then all we need to do is save $500–$1000 first. We can easily do this in a month. The quickest way is to hold a garage sale and start selling everything we don't need.

This serves two important purposes. First, we get our initial savings amount saved up so we can concentrate on paying off debt. Second, and this is the cherry on top, it gives us a physical representation of how many things we have. That helps give us an abundance mindset. When my wife and I started doing this, we realized how much

> **Sell so many things that your kids think they are next.**
> **—Dave Ramsey**

we had collected over the years we didn't even use. No matter how much stuff we sold, the more we looked, the more we found!

We saw we had so much; it was difficult to get rid of some things, and we had to donate and throw some things away. We also started to appreciate and be thankful for all the things we had. I encourage everyone to clean everything out. Try to minimize as much as possible. We'll see there's a lot to be thankful for, and on the plus side, we'll get some cash to put into savings and can help someone else in need when we donate.

Once we've saved that initial amount, we can start working on paying off debt.

When I first started trying to get out of debt, I failed to save a small amount. Instead, my wife and I had a credit card for emergencies. As luck had it, every time I made a small dent in my debt, an emergency came up, and we had to put it on that card, which put us back into debt.

That's the reason why this small savings is there. For the most part, minor emergencies are seldom more than $1,000, and if something like the car breaks down, we won't need to put the expense on a credit card.

If we have an emergency, we use the money and then save it again. We have to know what will constitute an emergency. A sale on a 55" TV is more than likely not an emergency.

Once we have that amount saved, we can start getting out of debt. If we don't have any debt and saved three to six months' worth of expenses, we can move on to investing.

Your Three to Six Months

Our first savings is a small safety net, so we don't dip back into our credit card for emergencies; this savings amount is for the big emergencies.

I pray we never experience anything tragic. However, sometimes things set us back. For those times, these savings will give us a cushion while we get back on our feet.

This amount needs to do three things:

- It needs to be accessible but not easily.
- Earn interest even if it's a little.
- Be your safety net.

We can do all three by placing this money is a money market, not a CD. Don't keep it in a regular bank. There's no place for it there. Why, you ask? Because of the fine print.

*Annual Percentage Yield (APY) is as follows: less than $50,000, 0.01%; $50,000 and over, 0.02%. APYs

That's from a major bank here in the U.S.

A money market acts as savings, but we get back some interest too, and it's liquid enough to withdraw if an emergency comes up. There are many money markets to choose from, but I usually recommend Ally bank. Their money market is super easy to set up and usually offer a high APY. I listed some more recommendations in the back of this book.

There are others that the APY goes as high as 2.05% or more. We can look into that, but usually, they have higher requirements. Some require us to have a minimum balance when others don't, so we might need to do a little shopping around and get one that works best for us.

Do research! The interest offered by different money markets will change. If we look into Citi right now, it will more than likely be different than the 2.05% I stated previously. Our job is to pick one we like with a high APY and stick with it. We don't need to chase higher APY every chance we get.

Other Savings

There are three different types of savings: Family savings, personal savings, and investment savings.

There's no need to get too detailed on these, but it's something I do, and it's helped me tremendously.

Family

Family savings are a small, short-term saving for the family like family trips, events, a new living room set, remodeling the home, or whatever will benefit the family.

This is shorter term and placed in a regular savings account. The only word of caution is to make sure we add extra into it. Because when it comes to family time, the calculations are never exact. That extra might come in handy on vacation.

Personal

When it comes to personal savings, I have one, and my wife has another. These are also short-term savings for each of us to save for our things. I like gadgets and technology, and she loves purses and shoes. Having individual savings, I can save for a new laptop, phone, or a bigger TV with surround sound speakers, and she can save for that costly purse she wants.

The reason why this helps so much is as a family, we have it all together, but it's a little difficult sharing a savings account when we don't care too much for the other's bigger purchases. If she wants a Louis Vuitton, well, she can save for it without it being in the same account I'm using to save for that new ultra-wide 80"TV.

College Fund

I'm not fond of the school system; college is no different. I strongly believe there's a reason to go to college and a reason not to go. If our kids want to become professionals, then, absolutely, college is necessary. But I also think college isn't the way to become wealthy or only way to be successful. Look at Michael Dell, CEO of Dell Computers, and Steve Jobs, who said quitting college was "one of the best decisions he has ever made," and many others.

The *get a college degree, get a good job dream* is a pipe dream. This is a fabricated lie to keep us as a tax-paying employee. So, unless we're going to get a professional degree, let's not spend money and get student loans with a degree that won't give us back a proper return on the investment. There's a reason this country has trillions in student debt.

With that being said, I started to put money into an investment vehicle explained later in this book for my two-year-old son. That way, by the time he graduates (he'll be homeschooled by the way), he'll have a nest egg large enough for compound interest to do its job, and he won't have to worry about his retirement and can focus on what he loves.

If he wants to be a professional, he's covered, or, if he wants to travel the world doing charity work, he's covered by living on the interest alone and will still have retirement when he's older.

We'll go over investments and how compound interest works in later chapters.

Investing

It should come as no surprise that one of the main things I'll be talking about is investing. This'll go right after we're out of debt and have our savings squared away.

There are multiple ways of investing, and we can do it with small or large monthly amounts. Savings for these more substantial investments are things like real estate, opening a business, buying a franchise, and the list can go on and on.

This type of savings is more longer-term, but not until retirement. For example, if we want to buy real estate, we know we need to save for the down payment. So, this will be the savings to do that. Yes, there are ways to get real estate without money, but that's for more savvy investors. Pick up a real estate book to learn more.

Bottom Line

Remember, we're not saving long-term; the only long-term is the emergency fund. But once we have our three to six months' worth, stop saving for it. We need to remember to replenish it if we do use it.

Another point I want to make is that the other types of savings are short-term, and we can save as much as we want. Figure out the amount of money we need and by what date, then do the math, and set recurring savings.

If we want that vacation next year, we need to make X amount to get the total cost. Let's say it's $3,000 (friendly reminder always to round up and add 10% for unexpected expenses). Let's say it's fourteen months away.

$$\$3,000 + \$300(10\%) = \$3,300/14 = 235.71$$
$$(\$240/\text{month rounded})$$

We can apply this to all of your short-term savings. I especially use it for birthdays and Christmas presents since I know they're coming up and by when.

Matthew 6:19 tells us, "Don't store up treasures here on earth, where moths eat them and rust destroys them, and where thieves break in and steal."

* * *

Next, we will put pencil to paper and start commanding our money where to go. Yes, I do mean making a budget. I know they may seem boring, and nobody likes making one. But I'm going to teach a way that will change everything. It was exceedingly difficult for me to stick to a budget, but I've been able to stay on target using this method, and now I command money where to go and not wonder where it went.

Action Step 8

Setup your savings!

Find a money market or savings account with a high-interest rate. There are a lot to choose from, but I understand that it can be a little nerve wracking. To give you peace of mind, you can't go wrong with any of the ones below. Just make sure that you are opening a money market. Some of them also have a checking account which you will also need in the next Action Step.

ally.com
citi.com
cit.com

If you have debt, save $1,000 in your emergency savings.

If you do not have debt, save three to six months' worth of income.

Make sure you open different savings accounts for emergencies, short-term, and investing.

Remember, the emergency savings is for that, an emergency. So, you will need to be aware of and ready to decide what constitutes an emergency if one were to happen.

SAVINGS ACCOUNT CHECKLIST

☐ Emergency   ☐ Personal

☐ Family   ☐ Investing

CHAPTER 18
FAITHFUL WITH A LITTLE

If you are faithful in little things, you
will be faithful in large ones. But if you
are dishonest in little things, you won't
be honest with greater responsibilities.
So if you have not been trustworthy in
handling worldly wealth, who will trust
you with true riches?

—Luke 16:10-11

We finally made it to the most loved and hated process, the budgeting, or as I like to put it, commanding my money what to do. Let me back up a little bit and say one thing. Remember when we talked about words being important? Well, this is where we can put that into practice. Don't think of it as a budget; think about this part as we are the master of our money. We are the ones in control! We will command it to do what and when!

As discussed earlier, we cannot be blessed with more if we can't control what we currently have. This is a set principle for all! The first thing a business needs to do is make a budget, gather all of their expenses and costs, straighten out their inventory, see their sales volume, and determine their profit after everything. How else will they be successful? If they don't know how much is coming in and how much is going out, it's impossible!

Running a home is no different. We need to know what's coming in and what's going out. It's simple addition and subtraction. As John Maxell puts it, "A budget is just telling your money where to go instead of wondering where it went."

Beyond all of that, we know and understand that God is a God of order and set principles. To experience true blessings, we need to have our finances in order also. If He moves in order, shouldn't we work within that as well? How much better would it be if we aligned ourselves with God?

Here is the problem. We all know we should do it, and some of us even start doing it, and then, we lose the momentum. We stop doing it, and we go back to our old ways. I have a fool-proof way to make budget long-lasting and straightforward. It's going to take about two to three months to get it all straightened out, but everything will be so much easier once it's in place. One key thing to bring up is it's not the *stop going to Starbucks* kind of budgeting. This is the *I command money! It does what I want!* type of budgeting.

We're the master, and money is the slave. This isn't about taking away our joy. If we find joy in a daily $10 coffee, we need to make a plan for it so we can command money to go toward that. However, before we can spend $300 on coffee, we need to meet certain needs.

Basic Needs First

Before everything, I want to make sure that we always, and I mean *always* take care of our four essentials for living.

- Food
- Shelter
- Clothing
- Transportation

These are essential to have every day! I can't tell you how many people would rather pay the minimum payment on a credit card instead of putting gas in their car or put off paying their rent because of other bills. Listen, the credit cards can wait if it means you're unable to provide our family's basic needs.

> If you have food in your belly, a roof over your head, clothes on your back, and a way to get to work tomorrow, you'll live to fight another day.
> — Dave Ramsey

To begin with, we shouldn't have gotten things on credit if we weren't able to afford it. I'm here to help us get out of this harsh and stressful situation.

I get a little passionate because I own apartments, and I have tenants who continuously pay late, but I see new TV or furniture boxes next to their trash can. A roof over our head is way more important than a new smart TV. But let's move forward.

The Math of Commanding

The first thing we need to do is the math. Sorry, there's no way around that. But don't worry, it's not going to be trigonometry. I don't care how much they taught it in school; we won't use it in regular life. Oh, but they didn't show us simple budgeting; that's why brother Rich is going to teach it.

We're going to keep it very simple. We can include many factors, but for the sake of simplicity, here's what we're going to do.

Income - Expenses = Zero

That's right. For the first time, we need to spend every single last penny we have but with a purpose. Here's how to do it. We begin by looking at our take-home income for the month (what we make after taxes). Before going to lunch on payday, what's the total amount of our checks?

Sorry if I am repeating myself, but this isn't the time to make excuses.

Okay, so we have a total of what we bring home a month. Good, now put that up at the top of your spreadsheet, and subtract tithe. The rest is used for our expenses. Now, we want to go down the list of all of our bills, mortgage or rent included, and debt minimum payments. We'll now subtract that from our income, but not before we subtract tithe.

Yes, I'll repeat it. It's the first of our income, not after we pay bills.

Proverbs 3:9-10 tells us, "Honor the Lord with your wealth, with the first fruits of all your crops. Then your barns will be filled to overflowing, and your vats will brim over with new wine."

It should be something like this:

Get To Zero

INCOME
- EXPENSES
ZERO

INCOME: $2,000

Tithe	- $200
Mortgage/Rent	- $700
Food	- $400
Misc (Gas, Light, Needs)	- $300
Debt/Savings/Investing	- $300
Whatever You Want	- $100
	$0

There are a couple of things to keep in mind with the above graph. Our living expenses should not be more than 50-60% of our income. If they are, it's time to minimize. We can't have a $500 car payment and a

$1,000 mortgage if we only have $2,000 in monthly income. I don't care how good we are in math; it won't work. I'm sorry.

When we have debt, our main priority is to get out of it. Depending on how aggressive we want to be, we might want to limit the "Whatever You Want" line until we're out. Then, we can reward ourselves by putting more into that bracket. Savings and investing should be a minimum 10% of income. Once our emergency savings is full, we can put it all toward income, and again, we can reward ourselves by putting a little more into our "Whatever You Want" column.

Side note: If our "Whatever You Want" is a nicer place or a car, that's perfectly okay. Remember, when we say yes to something, we need to say no to something else. Matthew 5:37 (NKJV) says, "But let your 'Yes' be 'Yes,' and your 'No,' be 'No.' For whatever is more than these is from the evil one."

Most of these will stay the same such as our mortgage and rent and most of our utilities. So, we can plan accordingly for those. There's a plan for everything! The main thing is, **You Command Your Money!**

COMMAND YOUR MONEY

But for the next two to three months, what we're going to want to do is take note of what we spend monthly. This will be the most excruciating three months if we aren't used to it. But it doesn't have to be. Every time we go to the store to buy groceries, toiletries, and gas, write it down on a simple spreadsheet. We want to have a total at the end of the month on what we spent on our home needs and groceries.

For the utilities, save some time and keep the bills for the next three months. It's a good habit anyway. In the end, we want an average of what we spend monthly for the following.

- Food, household needs, gas (Don't forget hair-cuts as I did)
- Utilities (light, water, phone, etc.)
- All Debt Payments

The Fun Part

Now, we get to the entertaining part. My wife thought I was crazy for this one. Let me tell you—it works so beautifully that budgeting will be a piece of cake.

The old budgeting method was doing what we discussed above and putting those amounts cash into envelopes, jars, coffee cans, or buckets. Well, those are a thing of the past.

We'll need five different bank accounts.

Yes, five, cinco. Three checking accounts and two savings. Now, this is the basic structure of how to do it. Afterward, I will show how I have mine setup.

The Five Bank Accounts purposes are as follows.

1. **Checking 1:** Rent, utilities, bills, and anything you can pay online.
2. **Checking 2:** Food, gas, and anything you pay in cash.
3. **Checking 3:** Entertainment such as eating out, going to the movies, etc.
4. Savings 1: Money Market (three to six months emergency)
5. Savings 2: Family

Real quick side note, when I told my wife about this, the first thing she told me was, "You can't even manage one bank account, and you want five?"

My account was continually in over-draft. It's not fun paying the bank $35 for a $2 burger because I only had $1.50 in the bank after a credit card payment went through, which was late, so there was a late fee.

Yeah, that was me.

As soon as I started implementing this Five Bank Account Strategy, all that was quickly over. And I can't wait for my readers to see their change in their lives. And when we get this done, please send me an email: myfive@ sheepamidwolves.com with the Subject: I got my 5.

How Does It Work

Before we open five bank accounts, we'll need a plan. It won't take long to make it, but it's essential that we don't end up with all these bank accounts and don't know how they work together.

First, we need to have our income or paycheck come into one central location. Since I have my own business, I have everything put into my business checking account. If we have a job, then it'll be our current bank account, and if we have direct deposit, even better.

Here's the trick, which is why I said it's going to take about three months to get it all squared away. But once we do this, we'll only need to worry about it once a month.

Here's what I mean. Teachers usually get paid once a month, so this will work super easy for them. It'll be a little harder for those who get paid weekly. The goal is to tell our money where to go on the last or the first day of each month.

So how do we do that? We will either need to pay some bills super early, and we might need to pay some a little late. I would prefer we do the former.

We usually pay our bills as they come. Whatever check that may be, that's what we use, but not anymore. Here's the quick method of doing it when we're paid biweekly. We already made a list of all our expenses, so we should know how much we can cover with one check by now. We will use one of our checks to pay our mortgage, and the rest will go into our budget for everything else.

Here's where the pain comes in, and the uncomfortable will strike. This is where we need to be willing to do what others won't, so we can live like others can't.

We'll need to cut out everything that isn't required, stop eating out, no more movies, and worst of all, pay bills twice in one month.

Before we go any further, we have to realize things worth it are never easy. There's going to be pain, stress, and uncomfortableness, so this is where I tell you to "Suck it up, buttercup." We are well on our way to being in a place where most people wish they were. Isn't it worth a little discomfort?

This is how I recommend we do it if we're living paycheck to paycheck. For the next two to three months, we'll need to start doubling up on our bills and paying the minimum on our credit cards. If our phone bill is $150 a month, give $300. If the light bill is $200, pay $400.

We have to understand this is a sacrifice we have to make. To be free, to be different, to no longer be where we're are at, we need to sacrifice and be uncomfortable for a short period. We can't reach success on a gravy train. This needs to get hard and challenging. This builds us up for resistance and strength.

If we need a second job, get a part-time job. If we need to sell more things, then sell more stuff. It's not the time to be faint-hearted. Do now what's hard, so it'll be easy later. I got a job at a Golden Corral, so no excuses.

Keep in mind if we can't put ourselves through this struggle for a short period, we'll live in a struggle for the rest of our life. We put ourselves in a hole, and now it's time to get ourselves out.

That's enough with the tough love; let's continue.

I say it will take about three months because I know we can't double up on all our bills in one month. We'll need to do one or two at a time. Once we double up on one, for the next month, we can pay only one month and double up on another. But don't stop the momentum.

By the third month, we want to be an entire month ahead of our bills.

But we're not out of the fire yet; once we're a month ahead, we need to go back and put pen to paper and separate everything according to how we pay for it.

Much like the bucket or envelope system, we need to put our money in the proper bank account. We can decide how we want to separate them, but this is how I have found the easiest way to do it.

My Five Bank Accounts

- **Bank One** (Checking)—Everything that is paid online, including mortgage/rent.
    - Ex. Light, Cable, Phones, Insurance, etc.
- **Bank Two** (Checking)—Everything I pay for in-person.
    - Ex. Groceries, Gas, Toiletries, Household products, Cleaning products, and everything you get that is needed monthly.
- **Bank Three** (Checking)—My entertainment and eating out
    - Note: Only after you are out of debt, my wife and I each have our own; this is up to you.
- **Bank Four** (Money Market)—Emergency Savings
- **Bank Five** (Savings)—Large purchases
    - Ex. Family vacations or other large family purchases.

I have a couple of other savings accounts, one each for my wife and myself, and since I have a business, I have a business account and a business savings account.

We need the five to start with, but once we get the hang of it, we can begin customizing our own.

So how do we work with all five? I use Google Pay and Zelle to transfer between banks since it's free and now you can set everything to be done automatically using Zelle. So, be sure to set that up. After that, we need one main one to receive our money. As I said before, I have a business, so all of my income comes through there.

But others will need to choose Bank One or Bank Two (I recommend our Bank One; it'll be more accessible this way, and well, I'm sure we already have that one setup with our direct deposit and bill pay). Bank One is where we'll be depositing all of our income.

Since we're already a month ahead in bills, we need to let the deposit come in and wait until the end of the month. We take our budget sheet and start dividing it between the rest of the accounts.

For example:

We receive a total of $2,000 in income; this is how we separate it.

Dividing into Your Accounts

BANK	INCOME OF $2,000
First Your Tithe	$200
Bank 1—All online bills	$1,000 + Min. Credit Cards + Snowball (pg. 163)
Bank 2—Groceries + Needs	$500
Bank 3—Whatever You Want	$0 if you have debt
Bank 4—ER Savings	You should at least have $1,000 then to CC
Bank 5—Large Savings	$0 if you have debt

We should already have all of these numbers from the budget sheet. If we don't have enough to meet our basic needs, then we have to go back and remove stuff and recalculate. We can't forget to factor in all our debt.

When we have debt, we have to pay that off first. In the following chapter, we'll discuss precisely how to do that. But for now, we want to factor in all the minimum balances of each debt.

Once all is in place, guess what? We can put all of our online bills on autopay using Bank One only. On the last day of the month, we'll move all of the rest of the money into our other banks. Therefore, autopay will take care of the bills for us without having to worry if we spent too much at the grocery store.

Now, it's even easier to set up automatic transfers to each of our banks, savings accounts, and investment accounts. Since we have done the math, we can set it up on the days we get paid until we can do it once a month. After that, it's just a matter of doing little quick checks on balances. This is way better than sitting in front of a computer and a stack of bills trying to see what goes where. Do it once, and then keep an eye on it.

Note: We need to make sure we're always leaving some wiggle room in our autopay bank one account, just in case the light bill is a little higher this month, or there's an extra charge on our cable or phone bill. I usually keep an additional $100 to be safe. Also, just because it's on autopay doesn't mean we set and forget. I make it a habit of going in twice a month to make sure we're on track, and all bills are paid accordingly.

We've made it this far, and we're a lot closer to being wealthy than 95% of the world. Congratulations! We've now started tithing, started a savings account earning us interest, and now we're the master of our money, commanding it what to do.

Unexpected Expenses

In a perfect world, nothing would ever happen, and our expenses would stay the same all year round. Unfortunately, things happen, and we need to be ready. Car registration, engine failure, medical expense—the list can go on and on. This is why we have the emergency savings account for these unexpected circumstances.

Extra Money

This is a nice little surprise to all of us when money magically appears. Either by a tax refund, birthday/ Christmas gift, a raise, or even a bonus from work. If we find ourselves with extra money, I first recommend we treat ourselves. We should buy something we've been wanting or go out to a fancy dinner. Then, save or invest the rest.

Two things we always want to consider is we don't want to be money-hungry with a tight grip on money, but we also don't want to squander it away. We should enjoy ourselves and then put the rest to work. We'll thank ourselves later. Remember, we want more assets that make more money, not material things that depreciate.

What If We Don't Make Enough?

This can happen a lot; we spend more than we make and can't keep up. It's okay. There are two solutions to this problem, and by this chapter, we should have already started the first one, which is to remove everything we don't need or use.

The second part of this is asking for a raise and/or my personal favorite, get a side hustle. This side hustle can be anything! We can even drive an Uber to generate some extra income.

There are other ways to generate extra income:

- Cut or maintain lawns on the weekends.
- Garage sale buy and sell on Ebay.
- Turn a hobby into a business.
- Teach something we're skilled in.
- Be a virtual assistant.
- Do freelance computer work (Add profile to Fiverr.com or Upwork.com).
- We can get paid to transcribe (https://www.rev.com/freelancers).

- We can even be a voice actor! (Check out voice. com)

With the Internet, there are a ton of other ways we can start generating some extra income right away.

* * *

The next chapter will cover what debt is and how to get out. It's based on a popular method often referred to as the snowball method. There are other methods, but I found that this is the one that worked for me when the others didn't.

Even without debt, it's wise to read the following chapter so we can understand how to get good debt properly for a little insight to help others.

Action Step 9

Command Your Money!

- List and separate your expenses into the categories below for each bank account and put a total amount to them.
- Be sure to add your debt if you have any and minimum payments to them.
- If you don't have debt, figure out an amount that works for your "Whatever You Want" amount
- Go open up checking accounts and set up automatic transfers to them with the amounts we have for each. This may take a while to get it just right. Stick to it! It will be worth it.
- Get to Zero.

CHECKING ACCOUNT CHECKLIST

☐ **Checking 1**—Everything that is paid online, including mortgage/rent.
Ex. Light, Cable, Phones, Insurance, etc.

☐ **Checking 2**—Everything you get that is needed monthly and paid in person.
Ex. Groceries, Gas, Toiletries, Haircuts, etc..

☐ **Checking 3**—Entertainment, Eating out, fun money
Note: Only after you are out of debt. My wife and I each have our own; this is up to you.

In total with your checking account and savings accounts, you should have minimum of five different accounts.

CHAPTER 19
CREDITOR LIKE THE DEBTOR

The rich rule over the poor, and the
borrower is a slave to the lender.

—Proverbs 22:7

I'd like two things to happen by the end of this chapter. I want to help as many people as possible become debt-free, and I want those people to hate bad debt as much as I do now. I say bad debt because I believe there's good debt, which I'll discuss later.

When we turn eighteen, credit card offers start rolling in the mail. It's amazing how these companies know. But we're not here to speak on marketing tactics; we're here to talk about bad debt.

Yes, there's good debt, and there's bad debt. I know Dave Ramsey doesn't believe in good debt, but the world and economy work on debt, and so should we—but only if we're wise enough to use it.

Not to worry, that's what we're going to discuss here.

We need to get rid of the bad debt. Bad debt includes high-interest store cards, credit cards, and even auto loans. There's a multitude of different types of debt, but we want to get rid of the following list:

- Credit Cards/Store Cards
- Bank Loans
- Money borrowed from relatives
- Past-due medical bills
- Student Loans
- Home Mortgage

Before we discuss eliminating debt, let's go back to the beginning of how debt started.

In the Beginning

It wasn't long ago when credit cards first emerged. If we think about it, that's why our grandparents never believed in debt. At that time, *putting things on credit* began, so it was relatively new to them.

Credit in the U.S was first introduced during westward expansion during the 1800s. Merchants used credit coins and charge plates to extend credit to local farmers and ranchers, allowing them not to make payments on their bills until they harvested their crops or sold their cattle.[16] This allowed them to continue doing business all year round. It wasn't exactly a credit card, but the concept was there. But it's not the type of credit we're talking about here.

Fast forward a century, and the first credit card was established in 1931 when American Airlines gave travelers the option to fly now and pay later. Diner's Club was created in 1950. However, this card was a way to pay for meals and was only available at participating locations. At that time, the card was used to charge food and pay for the tab at the end of the month.

Not even a decade later, in 1958, Bank of America busted out the first full-blown credit card. With it, the consumer could get what they wanted right away and pay small monthly payments until it was paid off completely, but with interest. Their method was to send mailers to California residents Bank of America cards. The system remains in effect today with the ability to apply for a first credit card that happens at eighteen.

Between 1958 and 1966, it was a fight to be on top. American Express expanded its reach by going to other countries and introducing the first plastic card in 1959. It was the perfect timing for IBC to introduce the magnetic strip. And it wasn't long before BankAmericard went national to become the nation's first licensed general-purpose credit card in 1966 and renamed it Visa in 1976.[17] Mastercard followed suit in 1966. Store cards didn't take long to start its credit cards, and the rest, as they say, is history.

Credit Debt Today

From that moment on, it grew into a beast. With the U.S having a total of $1 trillion in credit debt alone, $1.48 trillion in student debt, and more than 44 million borrowers in the nation and a combined total of $14 trillion.[18] What's happening is we're getting worse at handling debt because debt is getting easier to acquire. Now, even our smartphones have the option to apply for credit!

Apple has a credit card now! We've created a monster we continue to feed, and the sooner we stop and control it, the better it'll be. One of the best things I've done was get out of debt. When we use credit, we're stealing from our future self. It's money we don't have now, hoping we'll have it later.

Remember, I was horrible with money. Credit cards, bank loans, and borrowing from family were just as bad. I borrowed from three different places to purchase what I wanted. In several of my car purchases, I paid the car loan along with the money I borrowed for a down payment. I never intended to get out of debt; I kept piling it on. But at the same time, I hated paying so much for something I purchased months or years back.

Many credit cards have close to a 25% interest rate. But let's say we have a credit card with a $5,500 balance and an 18% interest rate. That costs $1,000 Annually! Over forty years, that's $40,000! Now let's say we invested that money at 12%. After forty years, we'd have earned $486,000. That new TV purchased with credit probably doesn't look good after forty years. Let's stop this vicious cycle; let's stop losing our money and giving it to the banks and financial institutions, and let's start making it work for us.

- Gold is the currency of Kings.
- Silver is the currency of gentlemen.
- Debt is the currency of slaves.

The Snowball

This is one of the most well-known methods of getting rid of debt. Honestly, I was skeptical at first. I started applying it, and after some time, I saw the benefit and momentum build. I wish I could say I was out of debt before I knew it, but it took a while, and it was work. However, the result was worth it.

The method is as simple as 1, 2, 3, 4.

1. Write down all of our debt from least to greatest (except mortgage).
2. Start knocking them down in that order by paying the minimum balance on the rest.
3. Put everything into that one until it's paid off.
4. Move on to the next one, carrying over what we were putting toward the previous one, and so forth.

For example, if the amount of our lowest debt is $500 with a minimum payment of $15, we should pay the $15 plus anything else we can add until the $500 is paid off. This is why it's important to first command our money where to go, because we will know exactly how much extra we can apply toward debt.

Once it's paid off, we take the total amount we were putting toward the first debt and add it to the minimum of the second and repeat. We keep adding the previous amounts to the next until they are all paid off. As you are moving toward the bigger debts, you will also notice that you will have a lot more to put toward it. Making it much faster to pay off those high balance ones.

There is a downloadable Excel sheet that will make it easy for you and also give you a debt free completion date.

I tried paying off the ones with the highest interest first but failed every time. It's one strategy and mathematically smart, but when we have a large balance and don't see any movement, it's discouraging. The snowball method will do several things. Because we'll feel a sense of motivation in paying off debt. It creates forward momentum to keep going to pay the rest off.

Once we are out of debt, we should go out and celebrate. We deserve it. Remember, after paying each card off, cut that card up, but don't cancel it. Where we're going, we won't need them anymore, but canceling a card will affect our credit score negatively. It's crazy how it works, but once we understand this, it'll make sense. A credit score is an *I love debt score.* The more cards we have in circulation with a consistently paid off-in-time balance, the better our credit score.

The main factors that go into how a credit score is calculated are [19]

- Payment history

- Amount of debt, credit limit compared to used credit
- Age of credit accounts also referred to as credit history
- Mix of credit accounts
- New credit inquiries

Notice how all of those have something to do with the amount and history of accounts. Large amounts of credit on multiple accounts paid on time over a long time equal excellent credit. Although there are credit cards with loyalty programs, points, and miles, I don't recommend focusing on that now. If we're in debt, obviously, we're unable to use them appropriately. Those cards work when we use them and pay them off in full before we get charged interest. A couple with children will pay an average of $1,382 in annual credit card interest charges.[20] That's how much we paid in interest for our 15k miles, which won't even buy us one round-trip ticket.

I waited to get out of debt. Then, I started using my card to accumulate miles with monthly purchases (gas, groceries, etc.) But before the credit company generates a statement, I pay it off in full. Putting everything on credit and not caring to pay it off in full every month took a long time and willpower to get it right. And old tendencies still creep up. Credit can be used for good, but credit cards with high interest need to be cut up, so they're not available at our fingertips.

There are only a few reasons why we'd purchase anything on credit when we shouldn't:

- We don't trust God to provide.
- We aren't content with what we have.

- We don't have the discipline to save and wait for it.
- And we're a slave to instant gratification.

The Good Debt

You were bought with a price; do not become slaves of men.
—1 Corinthians 7:23 NKJV

Yes, there is such a thing as good debt. The first thing to do is clean your credit and get your score up higher. I listed a couple of resources on doing it at the end of this chapter and book.

Once you are free from bad debt and have improved your credit score, you can start looking into getting good debt. There's a smart way of doing it. We need to follow certain principles. The last thing we want to do is borrow money only to have it not work out the way we thought and drop us back down into debt. Let me put it this way: the only debt people should be scared of is the one they need to work at a different job to pay it all back.

There are three basic things we need to consider if we'll be borrowing for investment:[21]

- The item purchased is an asset with the potential to appreciate or to produce an income.
- The value of the item equals or exceeds the amount owed against it.
- The debt is not so large that repayment puts undue strain on the budget.

One of the main questions we should ask ourselves is, *Will it produce an ROI (Return On Investment) higher than the repayment amount?* For example, in 2017, I borrowed $2,500 to pay for a mentor by the name of Gallant Dill. I had already been following him and knew who he was and what he was able to teach me. He was in a place I wanted to be, and I wanted him to mentor me so I could level up. So, let's take this loan and put it up against the three points from above.

I was purchasing an asset with the potential to help me and my business produce more income. My research led to multiple people who'd already been mentored by him and had increased their sales. There certainly was potential, not to mention the right knowledge will always appreciate. The people I spoke to had doubled, tripled, and even quadrupled their initial investment over a couple of months of mentorship. So, his mentoring exceeded the amount owed. $2,500 wouldn't put me in a hole if things went sideways, and the payments were $50 a month if I couldn't pay it off in a year.

I borrowed the money, and within two months of the mentorship, I made twice that money back. I paid off the loan, and even today, I continue to make money following what he taught me. Had I not borrowed the money, I'd still be making the pre-mentorship amount, and my business would've either gone stagnate or wouldn't have made it.

Widow and the Oil

In 2 Kings 4, we read a story about a young widow who's left with her husband's debt, and creditors wanted to take her two sons as slaves for payment. The widow in distress went before the king for help. To pay back her debt, the king instructed her to go to her neighbors and borrow empty jars of oil. Then in 2 Kings 4:3-4, he said, "Go, borrow vessels from everywhere, from all your neighbors—empty vessels; do not gather just a few; then pour it into all those vessels, and set aside the full ones." Then, in verse seven, he said, "Go, sell the oil and pay your debt."

I want to make this point if you didn't pick up on it. She didn't ask for the king's money, and the king didn't take matters into his own hands to lend it to her. The king didn't instruct her to borrow money from neighbors. He told her to borrow an asset that'd help her gather what she needed to sell and make money herself to pay off the debt.

With all that said, this story serves two purposes. One, when we want to get out of debt fast, we may have to sell things or get another source of income like a part-time job. A part-time job is not beneath us. It's a small sacrifice to be financially free. If we don't have enough income to put toward debt, we need to get a second part-time job; there's no other option. Our sole obligation is to pay off our debt. The story illustrates that we can acquire good debt as long as we meet the guidelines. Just like in my example, we can follow these to be sure it's a wise investment.

Be extra careful with investments while still in debt. They have to be no-brainers. For example, I had a friend who needed money and had too much debt. He was offered a seasonal job far away from his home but couldn't afford to pay for a hotel. So, he borrowed the money needed to stay somewhere and for food, but the job would pay him far more than what he originally borrowed. When the job was done, he could pay back the loan and get back on his feet. Notice that in both scenarios, paying off the loan was the very first accomplishment. This is exceptionally crucial. I know from experience.

Fixing Your Credit

Most of us have already ruined or have taken a hit on our credit report, and it needs to get fixed. It will become one of the greatest tools in your level up and create wealth tool belt. This is why it is so crucial that you start getting it repaired. We also need to know that credit bureaus are not in the business of keeping accurate records. They are for profit companies that are in the business of selling whatever records they have on us to the highest bidder. Yes, you read that right, Experian, TransUnion, and Equifax are for profit companies. Fun fact, Experian owns Burberry.

Their business model is simple.

- Collect your data
- Create a report and score based on your data
- Sell your information to the highest bidder

They sell credit reports and scores; they sell segmented information to debt collectors; they sell trigger data.

"After you apply for a loan, information about your application is sold by Experian, TransUnion and Equifax to various lenders that know you're actively looking for a loan and will target you with competing offers."[22]

If there are any inaccuracies, there are legal loopholes that allow you to improve your scores with relative ease. In a nutshell, repairing your credit is to force bureaus to report accurately by fixing and/or deleting any inaccurate accounts, which will significantly increase your scores.

Be aware that student loans, bankruptcy and child support are some that cannot be removed. Do not be fooled by "gurus" claiming they can have these removed from your credit report.

One in five people have an error on at least one of their credit reports.
—Consumer Finance Protection Bureau

In order for you to get started right away, here are three ways you can start working toward repairing your credit.

1) **Dispute Process**—With the dispute process it's simply going through the process of writing a letter to each bureau disputing negative information and / or accounts that are listed on your report. The bureaus are weary of "credit repair companies" sending letters on behalf of people so they have an automated process in which their AI systems read the letter and "validate" the debt. What you want to do is to hand write the letters in order to have a human being actually look at them.

2. **Pay to Delete**—If you have a small collection (anything that's affordable for you) and your intention is to simply pay back that debt, make sure you acquire a letter of deletion. Many debt collectors are shady and aren't even licensed to collect in your state. So, if you do not acquire a letter of deletion and send them money, there's a good chance they will leave it on your report and ignore your calls once they get their money.

3. **Debt Settlement**—Many debt settlement companies are charging you for something you can do yourself. If your debt is completely out of control and you can't keep up with it

any longer, what they'll tell you to do is stop making payments. Once your debts are about to go into collections, the debt settlement companies will negotiate on your behalf to settle for a lesser amount. Meanwhile, they are charging you monthly fees for a few years when that money could simply be going toward your debt. Be advised this method will ruin your credit but if you have no choice, it may be better than bankruptcy. Climbing out of this and repairing your scores is a lot easier than if you file for bankruptcy especially if you're looking to qualify to purchase a home.

One of my good friends has a DIY Credit Kit that will show you exactly how to get your score back up to where it needs to be. He has all the letters and a video walk through of steps to take to get it done yourself without paying someone. If it is overwhelming for you—which I know it was for me—he also provides a Done for You system. I will include his course at the end of this chapter as an action step, but before I do, I want to share with you one of his secrets to instantly boost your credit.

What you will need to do is become an authorized user of a credit card account from someone who you trust completely and trusts you completely. You can have them keep the card so they're not worried about you spending on their account.

This account(s) must have a minimum of two years of age (ideally four years+), perfect payment history, and low debt utilization (6% or less) on average, ideally with high limits.

In doing this you affect:

- Negative Items and Payment History
- Debt Utilization
- Length of History

Instantaneously . . . you could see a significant boost in a few short weeks (as soon as the creditor reports this account to your report).

Now this is a *short-term* trick, and it won't work very effectively if you have recent (two years or less) negative payment history, collections, etc.

If you want a more permanent solution, you need to know exactly how to influence and correct every aspect of your credit report.

Good Debt Turned Bad

As I've said before, I was horrible with money, but that didn't stop me from utilizing the opportunity to open up a business. I was quick to jump in with a friend of mine. However, I didn't have the money because I wasn't a saver, so I borrowed it. And I borrowed from everyone! Aunts, uncles, parents, and even my ex-brother-in-law. We were able to open on a bootstrap budget, but business started to boom. It was a bar in front of a college. This was before my walk with Christ, so I thought a bar was an excellent idea. I'm here to tell you it's not. But that's a different story.

I started making twice as much as I had before, and even though I had debts—car, Harley, some credit card, and, most importantly, new debt to open the business—I blew all of that money. Every time I got paid, I'd buy something new for me. I'd go out and eat more, and I'd

CREDITOR LIKE THE DEBTOR   173

take unnecessary trips. I didn't pay any of my old debt and much less any of the newly acquired debt.

Looking back at it, I could've paid off all of my debt, including what I'd borrowed from my family. Instead, I spent it on things I shouldn't have. After three years, the bar went from popular to old, and I stopped making the same amount of money, so we had to close it down, which left me with all the debt. I could've turned this into a good investment by getting entirely out of debt, but instead, it became even more of a liability. I took a considerable pay cut going back to a regular job, and I couldn't keep up with my debt. But I wasn't trying to get out of it. I kept borrowing. I hadn't learned.

Let's break down this investment and see how it stacks up when going through the list. A business can certainly have potential and be an asset, but many things can and will go wrong when it's the first go. It could've flopped right out of the gate. The research is there; not all businesses thrive.

I had no idea if it would work and if it would've covered the borrowed money. In this case, it would have, but not because I knew. It just so happened that way, but I didn't take advantage of it and lost everything and left in deeper debt. I borrowed $30,000 from multiple people, and there's no way to pay it back quickly. I was already $30,000 in debt, so if things didn't go right, I wouldn't have been able to keep up. Two years later, I had to start paying it off with very little income coming in.

We need to do our homework to see if we can pay investments back if everything falls apart. That's why it's always better to invest after we're out of debt. Eventually, I'd come to terms and start learning about money and finances. I started reading everything I could on how to work with money and fixing my financial state. I got rid of my car, sold my Harley (this one still stings), got a second job, and worked to get out of debt.

I urge anyone to do the same. In any financial decision, it's always good to consult God.

- Does this violate any Biblical principles?
- Is this mathematically sound?
- Do I have peace in my spirit about this?

Now, we should understand the difference between good debt and bad debt. I also pray we're well on our way to completely get out of bad debt and have insight as to the proper way to have good debt.

> Keep out of debt and owe no man nothing.
> —Romans 13:8 AMPC

* * *

In the next chapter, we'll start the exciting and wonderful world of investing. Even though I'm unable to put everything about investing in one book, I give an overview of the more popular methods and some resources to further our knowledge.

Now, let's start learning how to make your money work for you.

Action Step 10

Get rid of bad debt!

List all your credit card from least to greatest owed.

Start at the top and put everything you can toward that one, and minimal on the rest. After you pay off that one, start with the next one adding what you were putting on the first one to the minimum, and so forth.

There is a worksheet in the back of this book and an Excel file where you plug in the numbers, and you can plan out your snowball strategy, and it will give you a date of when you will be debt free.

Another thing that you need to look into is cleaning up your credit. A good friend of mine teaches on how to clean and boost your credit score. You can see his free video here: richcreditsolutions.com/free-video

Below is a free video of his Credit Repair Kit, but he also offers to do it for you, so you don't have to do everything yourself, saving you time.

richcreditsolutions.com/free-video

CHAPTER 20
REAPS WHAT HE SOWS

Invest in seven ventures, yes, in eight;
you do not know what disaster
may come upon the land.

—Ecclesiastes 11:2

This is one of the longer chapters in this book, so be prepared for the water hose effect. It'll cover an overview of most of the different types of investments we need to be familiar with. And it'll cover assets we can start acquiring to build our wealth. Let's get down to business.

After saving, budgeting, and getting out of debt, we're in a place where we're free but not out of the woods yet. Investing has to become part of our life.

There are a few ways you can earn or save your way to a fortune that everyone can do. However, there is a way we can all create wealth in the long term—make money your slave. Anyone can do it through multiple businesses, but the other way to do it is to invest.

If you do have a business or businesses, you should still have money working for you that does not require having employees, a building, or moving parts, and will only take a couple of minutes a couple of times a year.

Before we do, a rule of thumb is all of our expenses, including mortgage, utilities, taxes, insurance, and anything else shouldn't exceed 50%–60% of our income. This means 10% is going to tithe, and the other 30-40% will be to give and invest.

Some of us might be at that point where investing is a gamble or something we don't need to do. There's nothing worse than having our money stored up in a bank and watching it dwindle under inflation.

The 2018 **inflation rate** was 2.44%. The **inflation rate** from 2018 to **2019** was 1.75%.[23]

That means that if our money is in a savings account or under our mattress, it's losing value. We need to stay ahead of the average 2% to have the same amount as when we started. Investing is the only way.

The Three Servants

Let's use the parable in Matthew 25:14–15 to illustrate, "For it is just like a man about to go on a journey, who called his own slaves and entrusted his possessions to them; to each according to his own ability."

Man 1: Five Talents (bags of gold)
Man 2: Two Talents (bags of gold)
Man 3: One Talent (bag of gold)

Just to add some perspective, a Talent: One-gram **costs** about $38. At this **price**, a **talent** (33 kg) would be **worth** about $1,400,116.57

In Matthew 25:16–18 (NKJV), we learn more about their talents. "Then he who had received the five talents went and traded with them and made another five talents. And likewise, he who *had received* two gained two more also. But he who had received one went and dug in the ground and hid his Lord's money."

> Each was given a different amount according to their ability, if you can't handle a little how can you be expected to handle more? He who is faithful with a little is faithful with a lot.

Then, in Matthew 25:19 (NKJV), "After a long time, the lord of those servants came and settled accounts with them."

Man 1: Master, you entrusted five talents to me. See, I have gained five more talents.

Master: Well done, my good and faithful servant; you were faithful with a few things. I will put you in charge of many things.

Man 2: Master, you entrusted two talents to me. See, I have gained two more talents.

Master: Well done, my good and faithful servant, you were faithful with a few things. I will put you in charge of many things.

Man 3: Master, I knew you to be a hard man, reaping, where you did not sow and gathering where you scattered no seed. And I was afraid and went away and hid your talent in the ground. See, you have what is yours. (In this day it would be like putting it into a regular savings and making an interest of .0000000001%)

Master: You wicked, lazy slave. You knew that I reap where I did not sow and gather where I scattered no seed. So you ought to have deposited my money with the bankers, and at my coming I would have received back my own with interest. (I am going to say there were no money markets in Jesus' time, but you get the idea)

Therefore, take away the talent from him and give it to the one who has the ten talents. For everyone who has more shall be given, and he will have an abundance; but from the one who does not have, even what he does have shall be taken away. (Remember this as we will talk about it later)

Let's Invest. But in What?

I hope by now, we're open to investing. But some of us are probably wondering where to start. There are a ton of options, but we're going to cover the good ones.

We'll be covering the following types of investments:

- Self
- Business Venture
- CDs
- Stocks/Bonds/Mutual Funds/Index Funds
- 401(k)
- IRAs and Roth IRAs
- Annuities
- Life Insurance
- Real Estate

This is a brief introduction to each of the types of investments. Each one of them can go into deep rabbit holes, but I want us to at least be aware of them. Once we start to invest, we should do some research and learn more about the investment. Proverbs 19:2 tells us, "It is not good for a person to be without knowledge, and he who hurries his footsteps errs."

Words To Know

The purpose of this book is to be aware of what's out there and become financially free. This isn't an investment book. Before we get into it, here are a couple of words to know.

Diversification: spread your investments around, different sectors and multiple markets

Risk Return Ratio: greater risk greater return (think savings to Vegas)

Inflation: a situation of rising prices in the economy (4.2% over the last seven years, if we factor in taxes and we'd need 6% to stay ahead)

Liquidity: how quickly we can get the money; checking is liquid vs. home equity

Brokers: Are sales agents who trade securities for their clients earning a commission on each trade. They also provide services for their clients, such as trading advice and tips on opening and closing prices.

Bull Market: When the market goes up, the economy is booming. A way to remember is; bulls attack their prey from the bottom up. If you have ever seen matadors, you will notice that they buck up with their horns.

Bear Market: This is when the economy takes a hit, and it's going down, such as the dot com bust in 2000, 911 in 2001, Housing Crisis in 2008, and the Crash of 2020. A way to remember is bears attack from the top down, as they stand on their back legs and claw lower.

Compound Interest: Interest calculated on the initial principal, which also includes all the accumulated interest of previous periods of a deposit or loan. It adds up slowly then spikes. The way it works in basic terms is like: If we took a single penny and doubled it every day, by day thirty, we'd have $5,368,709.12. That's the power of compound interest.

Investing

Self-Investing

This doesn't mean playing the lottery. While I'm on the subject, the lottery is, by far, the worst investment ever. It'd be better to go to Vegas and gamble. The odds are better. I wouldn't recommend that either, but it's a point I needed to make. The average American spends $250 a year on lottery tickets; the scary part is there is a one in 300,000,000 chance of winning. I guess "chance" isn't the best word to use there.

Let's now put those $250 into an investment. The stock market over twenty years will earn us about $12,000 with those $250. That's $12,000 instead of, well, nothing. The odds are against us in the lottery. With the same $250, we can also treat our family to several nights at the movies. It buys a lovely anniversary dinner, maybe even two beautiful date nights with the wife, and even some concert tickets.

Best of all, we can buy ten to twenty books from Amazon or 200 books from the library or used bookstore for self-investment, which can turn into more.

Warren Buffett says, "The best investment you can make is an investment in yourself."

I've bought many books that've helped me learn and have contributed to my income. They've also provided me with all this knowledge in this book and more to come.

Learning doesn't stop when we leave high school or graduate college. It's a continuation. Most of the things we learn outside of

> Be patient with yourself. Self-growth is tender; it's holy ground. There's no greater investment.
> — Stephen Covey

those four walls will further our knowledge. Learning and growing daily is the best thing we can do. It'll forever be the wisest investment we can make. Everything else can be taken away in an instant, but no one can take away our knowledge. We're reminded of this in Proverbs 16:16, "How much better to get wisdom than gold, to get insight rather than silver!"

Give Yourself a Raise

Remember when we spoke about needing extra money in a previous chapter? This is how we start if we don't know what to do. Investing in ourselves will open the doors to making extra money and eventually even quitting our day job if we want to. It's true what they say, "The more you learn, the more you earn." Self-investing is all about growing and building skills we can turn into a career. If we've always wanted to learn how to make websites, we can learn and sell websites to businesses and individuals. If we've always wanted to learn how to build cabinets and furniture, we can learn to build and sell them!

If we already have a skill, we only need to monetize it. How do we do that? Learn how then apply. Information is power when we put action into it. If we know something others don't, great; teach people and charge them. Anyone can learn a skill, especially if they have a passion for it. This is what it means to grab the bull by the horns and make the life we want. Creating multiple streams of income is the greatest thing we can do to level up. Don't forget, just as we are created in the image of God; we are creators.

Business Ventures

Genesis 2:15 tells us, "The Lord God took the man and put him in the garden of Eden to work it and keep it." When it comes to business ventures, the list can go forever. We now have the power of the Internet to start a business from the comfort of our home and work on it while we maintain a job. There are many to choose from. We can also join a multi-level marketing venture (MLM) to guide us, or even save up for an already-established franchise. While I'm not an advocate of MLM, I know several people who've made a nice living from it, but they do put in a lot of work into it.

We know for sure we want to start a business as though we're planning on franchising it. We want to build a system where it's a cookie-cutter process. The reason I say that is we eventually want to work *on* the business and not *in* our business. Proverbs 11:26 (NKJV) tells us, "The people will curse him who withholds grain. But blessing will be on the head of him who sells it."

The difference is simple; when we work in our business, it turns into a job where we have to go. We could start with excitement and passion, but sometimes, that passion wears off, and we're stuck. Now, this doesn't happen all the time. Some people work in their business, and they couldn't be happier. All I'm saying is wouldn't it be better to have the option?

Compound Interest Power

Albert   Einstein says, "Compound interest is the eighth wonder of the world. He who understands it, earns it; he who doesn't, pays it."

I briefly went over how compound interest works but is it in the Bible? Well, it's all in the numbers. First, we need to understand the Law of 72. Simply put, it's how long it'll take for our investment to double, depending on the interest earned.

So, let's say we have $5,000 invested, and it's earning us 10% interest.

$$72 \div 10 = 7.2$$

Our investment would double every 7.2 years and keeps compounding. Meaning it's now using the previous amount to double every 7.2 years ($5,000, $10,000, $20,000, $40,000 and so on).

This is a very simple understanding of compound interest, but it's worth a lot to know it. On a side note, one thing we need to understand is the Hebrew language is also characterized as numbers. So, for a second, let's take a look at the number nine or tov, which means *good* or *truth*. It's a symbol of completeness of God and also a symbol of finality. When God finished one of His creations, He always said it was good.

As we learned in earlier chapters, we need to see the abundance in all things. We live in an abundant world, and eight is the Biblical meaning for new beginning or eternal life, and is symbolized as infinity or abundance. Just turn the eight on its side, and we'll get the ∞ infinity symbol. The coolest thing about this is if we count all the times gold is mentioned in the Bible, the total amount is eight. To go one step further, the eighth time God creates something and says it's good, it's gold! Not only is it good, but it's also abundant!

Now, let's take the abundance of everything, multiply it with everything that's good and true; it gives us what we refer to as the eighth wonder of the world, or compound interest.

8 X 9 = 72
Abundance X Truth = Compound Interest

Yes, it's important! Most importantly, we understand it works on time. Lucky for us, *Business Insider* did the math for us in the following:

They took three different investors and tracked their investments and the time they started.

Investor 1 starts at the great age of 25 and puts in $300 a month for a total of $144,000.

Investor 2 doesn't start investing the same amount until age 35 for a total of $108,000.

Investor 3 has a late start at age 40 and wants to catch up so he doubles up and puts in $600 and puts in more money than Investor 1 and 2 for a total of $180,000.

> *Our first investor, who began saving at 25 and, after all the compound interest takes effect, will have a balance of about $460,000 when ready to retire at 65.*
>
> *Meanwhile, our second investor has only about $251,000 in her account at retirement age. Missing out on those ten years of interest means that our second investor will retire with about 55% as much money as our first investor.*
>
> *The last even though they put $36,000 more into her account than the first investor, she ends up with just $359,000 at 65, about $101,000 less than the early investor.*[24]

For those of us who like seeing graphs, here is a visual representation of compound interest provided by Providened.

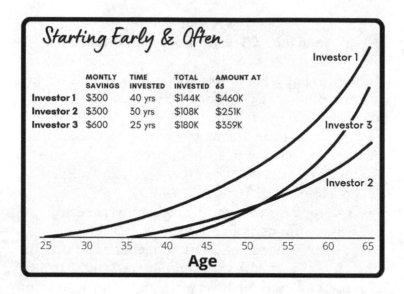

	MONTLY SAVINGS	TIME INVESTED	TOTAL INVESTED	AMOUNT AT 65
Investor 1	$300	40 yrs	$144K	$460K
Investor 2	$300	30 yrs	$108K	$251K
Investor 3	$600	25 yrs	$180K	$359K

As we can see, starting even ten years late will have a significant difference. Starting fifteen years later, investor 3 still couldn't catch up by doubling his monthly savings. The sooner you start the better, you can take advantage of compound interest and get more return in the end, without having to play catch up and putting more in. It's another reason why I'll start my son's account as an investment instead of a savings.

CDs

Don't do them. We might as well put our money in a money market where it's still liquid and earns about the same in interest.

Stocks/Bonds/Mutual Funds

Typically, when someone mentions investing, this is the first thing we think. Let's cover them quickly to have some knowledge and decide what path we'd like to take and how to start.

Stocks and the Market

Think of stocks as a bunch of different snacks you can go and buy from a store like Sam's or Costco; you have all different types with all kinds of flavors and options. The store represents the stock market, Sam's and Costco are the NYSE (New York Stock Exchange) and NASDAQ (National Association of Securities Dealers Automated Quotations).

With all of the different snack types to try, companies have made it easier with variety packs. We now have different types of variety packs such as chips, sodas, candies, etc. Just like there are separate sections, called sectors of stocks, which are Technology, Financial, Energy, Retail, and on and on. Within each sector, you find individual companies. For example, in technology, you will find Google, Amazon, Apple, and all the tech companies. Just like a variety pack of soda, you find grape, citrus, etc.

In the most basic of terms, a share of stock represents legal ownership in a business. It is a tiny piece of the company that we own and get back when and if the company does well. The amount of each share is congruent with the value of the company. If the company's value goes up, so does the value of each share.

In our example, the store would be the New York Stock Exchange; they have all of these variety packs to choose from. Let's say chips as your variety pack and Doritos cool ranch as your chips. The Doritos cool ranch in this example is what we would refer to as a single stock. Now, let's say you grabbed your top favorites from each variety pack and put them together.

So, you now have cool ranch and Cheesy Cheetos from the chips, Dr. Pepper from the soda, Snickers and Twix from the candies, and a small peanuts bag. You put these all together, and you just made a gift basket of your top favorites. This is called your portfolio!

Unfortunately, if we don't know what's out there, it's hard for us to build our portfolio. It's like making a gift basket for someone else. We could get our favorite things we love and use every day. This is what most people do, and it's a good strategy for the long run, especially if you get big billion-dollar companies.

The cool thing is that some gift baskets have already been created for us, with the best "most popular" stocks already in them called indexes. So, you can buy a single stock or an index, which would be a gift basket with all the best companies.

The U.S. stock market comprises three major indexes: the S&P 500, Dow Jones, and the Nasdaq Composite. Whenever you hear about the market moving up or crashing, it is referring to these three.

At the top is the most referred stock market indicator called the DJIA (Dow Jones Industrial Average) or Dow for short. It includes thirty largest, most traded stocks in the United States, including 3M, American Express, Boeing, Walt Disney, IBM, Walmart, and 24 other well-known companies that we all know and love. You will hear about the Dow most when watching the news.

Next is the S&P 500 (Standard & Poor's). Don't let the name fool you. This index includes 500 of the top companies. It's deemed the best gauge of the overall market because it accounts for about 75% of all U.S. stocks.

Unlike the DIJA and S&P, the Nasdaq Composite Index financial journalists and reporters often quote more than 3,300 stocks. It has a baby sister named Nasdaq 100, which holds, you guessed it, 100 largest companies in the market and are mostly all in the technology sector and have companies outside of the U.S.

I will show you later in this chapter how you can be a part of the entire market by investing in these major indexes. For now, let's talk a little more about single stocks.

Single Stocks

Following our previous example, let's say you only want Cool Ranch Doritos and nothing else. Well, you can in the form of a single stock. This is when you purchase single or multiple shares of a company. This is the form that many think they can hit the stock lottery, buying shares of one company, and then that company skyrockets.

It would be similar to buying that bag of Doritos for $0.50 back in 1990, saving them and selling them today for $1, and keeping the profit. Or the luck of the draw and all cool ranch was no longer made, and your bag is now worth $50.

For example, Apple hit a low in 1993, but by 2011, a $23,000 investment would be around $350,000. Jeff Besos is leading the world with Amazon, and if we had invested even $1,000 during Amazon's IPO in May 1997, our investment would be worth $1,341,000 as of August 31, 2019.[25] Even closer to home, investing $1,000 in June 2010 would've made us $16,867. Not bad for a $1,000 initial investment.

With few exceptions, the captial raised by the shareholders doesn't have a date by which it must be repaid, nor a guaranteed dividend rate. This means it acts as a cushion for a company's lenders.[26]

Single stocks are UN-diversified, solely for the reason we'll have only invested in one company; if that company goes under, so does our money. If we do invest in single stocks, the best words of advice I can give is to pick ones we love. Not one you heard about from your father's brother's nephew's cousin's former roommate that saw it on the Internet.

Think about single stocks like a sports team. We follow them, root for them, but even if they lose a game, we might be disappointed, but we never lose our faith in them. Remember, a single stock is a piece of the company, so we need to pick one we want to be a part of. The only thing different in stock is if our team wins, so do we.

There are two types of single stocks to be aware of.

Common Stock: these are the stocks to which everyone is referring to when they talk about investing in stocks. They are directly proportionate to the share of a company's profits or losses. A Board of Directors, that are elected by the stockholders, decide whether to retain those profits or send some or all back to the stockholders as cash dividends, physical check, or electronic deposit that is forwarded to the brokerage or retirement account that holds the stock.[27]

Preferred Stock: is where shareholders receive a specific dividend at predetermined times. Both are single stocks and should be handled the same—pick ones we love, and don't put all our eggs in one of these baskets.

Cashflow with Single Stocks

Ever hear the term "buy low sell high?" This is probably the best example and something I love doing. The process is creating cashflow through of stock trading. Need another idea on how to get more income? This is a skill anyone can learn. It takes some time and a lot of patience. In its most basic form, we buy stocks to sell them at a higher price and make a profit. When the stock goes down, we buy more and sell it again at a higher price for more profit. There are many books on this subject, and I'll list my favorite at the back of this book.

Bonds

A bond is a debt by which a company owes us money. This means instead of buying a piece of a company, like a stock, we're loaning a company (or government) money. Same as a stock, it will go up or down according to the company's performance, but along with current interest rates. Not all bonds are created equal, and are still considered high risk. This is because the company's ability to repay the investment we put is all depending on their performance. Usually, government bonds are a bit more secure, but still on the higher risk scale.

Mutual Funds

Mutual funds are a collaboration of a bunch of different stocks in different companines. So, one mutual fund will have smaller portions of different single stocks. For example, American Funds The Growth Fund of America A (AGTHX) owns lots of tech giants: Facebook (FB), Microsoft (MSFT), and Amazon (AMZN) are the fund's top three holdings.[28] It does the diversification for us in a single stock. Most mutual funds are actively manageed, meaning they have a professional portfolio manager managing the fund, by picking and choosing the companies they think are best. Keep in mind that this does two things. There will be a higher cost because it is actively managed, and just because there is a "professional" does not mean it's better. In reality, professionals hurt the fund more than help it.

Index Funds

Index funds are another type of mutual fund that aim to track the performance of a specific market index such as the S&P500 or Dow Jones and are my absolute favorite to invest in. We can find their ETF (Exchange-Traded Fund) on any brokerage and invest and trade it like a regular stock. The price of the fund will go up or down as the entire index goes up or down. Unlike mutual funds, Index funds typically have lower costs because the portfolio manager doesn't have to make as many investment decisions.

I prefer Index Funds as it follows the index, and we don't have to pay the fees a mutual fund would charge. A mutual fund is pretty much trying to beat the market and charging you for it. Here is the problem; no one can beat the market! And as they say, if we can't beat them, join them!

These are currently some of the ones I invest in. Again, I'm not a financial advisor. As always, research and invest responsibly. These are simply for you to get started an on the rigth foot. There are plenty more out there.

- **SPDR Gold ETF Trust (GLD)** - Cost effective way for indirect exposure to gold
- **SPDR S&P 500 ETF Trust (SPY)** – Tracks S&P 500; 500 Large and Mid Cap Companies
- **Invesco ETF Trust (QQQ)** – Tracks Nasdaq; 100 Largest Companies in Tech Sector
- **Invesco S&P Equal Weight ETF (RSP)**– Like SPY but equal distribution between companies

- **Vanguard Total Stock Market ETF (VTI)** – Diversified; 10 top companies and securities
- **ARK Innovation ETF (ARKK)** – Actively managed; long term growth
- **Vanguard International Equity ETF (VT)** – Developed and emerging markets

Pro Tip for Investing: The most important thing I can recommend when investing in any stock, mutual fund, or index fund is always invest slow and steady over time and only what is affordable, and don't be greedy. It's for the long haul.

For example, if we have $10,000, we don't want to invest all of it at once. We want to do it often and not as one lump sum, so divide it up and invest in the same stock weekly or biweekly. This is best practice whether we're in a bull or bear market. The same concept goes if we can afford $100 a month. Invest it every month, whether the stock is up or down. This gives maximum coverage and, over time, gives a better return. Remember, we can't predict the markets, so we don't know if or when it'll go up or down. This strategy works best.

> Bulls and bears make money, but pigs get slaughtered.
> —Jim Cramer

How to Invest in Stocks and Index Funds

When I was younger, I always wanted to invest in Google. I loved Google back then, and I still do! The price in 2004 was about $50 a share, and I had two things working against me. The first thing against me was myself; I couldn't save for a haircut, much less purchase a stock. By the way, the price as of this writing in 2020 is $1,500 a share. Even one stock would've given me $1,450. Imagine if I put my tax returns into Google? But no, I thought that 72" screen TV I eventually sold for $200 at a garage sale was way better.

The second thing against me was not knowing where to start. Even though we had Google, getting a brokerage account wasn't as easy as today. There are a ton of options now available! Many of them are even free and take ten minutes to set up and another two minutes finding the stock or ETF we like and investing in it!

We can own shares of Walmart, Johnson and Johnson, Apple, Tesla, Google, Amazon, whatever we want. The list goes on and on! Plus, some of these pay dividends! We get a cut depending on how many shares we have. The company grows, and we get paid, some on a quarterly. I've used a lot of different brokerage accounts looking for the best one.

Here are some I like: and depending on your level which one to get.

Absolute Beginner

If we're beginners, we don't know anything more than what we previously read but want to start ASAP! My best recommendation is using Acorns. (Link: https://bit.ly/saw-acorns) Acorns is super easy to setup. It asks how conservative or aggressive we want to be, and it creates an entire investment strategy. All we have to do is connect it to our bank, choose if we want to deposit manually or automatically, and if we want to invest the round-up cents from every transaction. Everything else is done for us. The current cost is $1 a month or $3 if we want the Acorns later, which is a Roth IRA. This is a set it and forget it and an excellent starting investment account with no effort. It also has *found money* which works with several online vendors, such as Walmart, Airbnb, and others by giving you a dollar amount or percentage of a purchase you make.

Starter

If we know what stocks or ETFs we want to buy or if we want to explore but don't have the experience, I highly recommend Robinhood. (Link: https://bit.ly/invest-robinhood) This is a great way to explore in the picking and investing stocks and ETF world. We can also trade. If we buy one stock for $5 and it shoots up to $15, we can sell it and make a $10 profit. It has some news info and brief fundamental analysis for each company. This one is currently free, but we have to put in the manual work of picking and buying. Trading stocks is risky and is best to learn and practice the skill before you jumping in.

Once we gain some more expierence I highly recommend moving over to a larger brokerage like TD Ameritrade, Fidelity, or Charles Schwab. Open one up and start learning how to use it so we can eventually move everything over to them.

We want to start investing right away and those have a bit of a learning curve so we don't want to get discouraged.

Intermediate to Advanced

If we're at this level, we don't need the run-down of each of the following. These are some I currently use and what I use them for.

TD Ameritrade Think or Swim—https://bit.ly/invest-tdts

I use this one for my ETF investing. I buy ETFs monthly and leave them for the long haul.

Webull—https://bit.ly/invest-webull
I use this one for trading. I love their interface on mobile and desktop. It's super customizable and easy to use for daily and swing trading. It also has a nice community to be a part of, and the cool thing is, we can trade paper money (fake money) to get used to it before we lose any real money.

M1 Finance—https://bit.ly/invest-m1
I use this one much in the same way as TD Ameritrade. The difference is with this one is we set up our own "mutual fund." We can make what they call a pie and make slices filled with whatever stocks or ETFs we want. If we want our pie to consist of all the major players like Amazon or Google but don't have $1500-$2000 per share of each, we can put them into our pie and buy fractions of the company. We can decide what percentage of each goes to give to them by only investing small amounts at a time.

Public—https://bit.ly/invest-public
This one is more fun than anything. It's a little community where we can buy fractions of individual stocks. Unlike M1 Finance, where we make a pie with slices, we can go to a stock, and no matter the share price is, we can buy a small fraction of it. I use this one for the big stocks I want to have full shares of but don't want to put $1,500 on one share all at once. For example,

for Google or Amazon, I can put $1-$200 at a time until I have a full purchased share.

Interactive Brokers—https://bit.ly/invest-interactive
I don't know too much about this broker, but I thought I would list it here because it is one that can be used overseas unlike the other ones.

There are so many others to choose from, and most of them are starting to be free. Like anything else that involves money—we should do our research to see which ones we like and are most comfortable with.

I am going to repeat this again, as we are learning, pick a larger brokerage and start learning how to use it. We will want to eventually move over all our holdings to them. Although Robinhood, Acorns and others are insured, we want to hold our long term portfolio in a brokerage that has been around a longer time.

Happy investing in the stock market!

Many Others

The list of different investments and funds can fill a book. The general idea here is to show the main ones and give some information on each. With everything, we need to practice safe investing and do our due diligence for each. The main thing to consider is how to invest responsibly in each. When it comes to mutual funds, we want to diversify as well. Diversify the diversified. And it all depends on how aggressive we want to be.

The best practice is to diversify over four different kinds of mutual funds and some index funds.

- **Growth**—Companies in a growth stage (mid-cap funds)
- **Growth and Income**—Large, well-established companies (large-cap funds)
- **Aggressive Growth**—Small active, emerging companies (small-cap funds)
- **International**—Overseas funds

As I said, depending on how aggressive we want to be, we still need to pick out the right ones for us. Here's a quick guide on what to look out for when choosing a fund.

- Always look at the track record, performance the past five years
- The longer, the more reliable.
- Don't buy one less than five years old.
- Track record around at least 12% (S&P 500 historical Average).
- From 1926 to 2010, it had an average of 11.84%.
- Just remember, nothing less than 7%.
- This is money that will be invested long term

Warren Buffett says, "Wide diversification is only required when investors do not understand what they are doing."

What about Market Crashes?

Market crashes are one of the main reasons people are scared of buying stocks. They don't want to invest in stocks, bonds, or mutual funds because they're afraid there'll be a stock market crash, and they'll be left with nothing. Can it happen? Yes, but we'd have to keep in mind one main important thing. It's not our money, and we can't solely depend on it! I'm not saying be careless, but let's take a look at history.

This is a small list of crashes that have happened since the beginning of the stock market.

- Wall Street Crash of 1929
- Recession of 1937–38
- Post-WWII 1946
- Kennedy Slide of 1962
- October 1974
- Black Monday 1987
- Friday the 13th 1989
- Early 1990s recession
- Dot-com bubble 2000
- September 11 attacks 2001
- Stock market downturn of 2002
- Financial crisis of 2007–08
- And as I am writing this, the market has just taken a dip because of The 2020 Market Crash

100 Years Dow Jones History

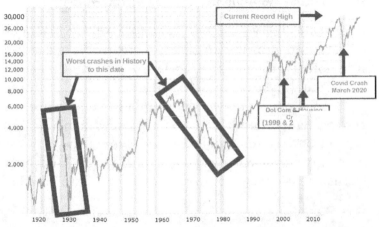

We've been through quite a lot of crashes over the past century. Crashes happen every five years, with major ones every ten and lasting up to a year. When most crashes drop, about 33%, larger ones can drop 50%. But here is the thing, you don't lose any money until you sell your shares, and people don't sell their shares unless they get scared. But notice a pattern? Every bear market always goes back up.

Take a quick look at the chart above. Just before 2010, we had the financial crisis of 2007-08. People took their lives, and some said we would never recover. Now, take a look at what happened right after that. Just like the Great Depression and the Dot Com Bubble, there was an explosion upwards of more than 70%! If people hadn't sold and stayed in the game, the market has increased by 250% since then. Over the past two decades, the average return has been 10% -12%. The stock market will always be good news; the secret is to get in as early as you can and don't let fear control you.

> Buy when there's blood in the streets, even if the blood is your own.
> — Baron Rothschild

TRS (Teacher Retirement System) or the 403(b)

I want to take a moment here to give my teachers, private non-profit, and government workers a quick side note. Don't solely depend on your TRS (Teachers Retirement System) or a 403(b).

I don't care what the department says; it's not the best retirement fund. If we weren't forced to be in it, I'd say get out! Here's a quick why. In some states, these plans give an average of 2.3% return, but if we have learned anything, we know that we have 1.75% inflation and taxes to stay ahead of. That's already 5-6% of what we're earning or more! We've also talked about the average market return is 11%. And all they are doing is putting it into the market via mutual funds. That means they are paying out 2.3%—enough for us to pay the inflation—and they're keeping over 8%!

This also includes 457 plans given to state and local government employees. Please be aware of where your money is going, how much your return will be because it might not be what you are expecting, and by the time you find out, it may be too late. Remember, we want to pay less than 1% in fees and get at least a 7% return. Our future self will thank us.

I can't stress this enough; please invest elsewhere. The last thing we want to do is retire and still have to work part-time so that we're able to make ends meet.

The 401(k)

I'm going to make this as short as possible because I don't like the idea of the 401(k), but for most Americans, this is the only investment they're a part of. Most of the time, it's not by choice but because of their employers. Let's go back in history to see how this all started.

There was a prolonged recession in the 1970s. This long, deep recession was caused by the quadrupling of oil prices and high government spending on the Vietnam War.[29] This led to "stagflation" and high unemployment. The Stock Market was going down, and companies were losing money. And due to the previous depression, people were scared to buy-in. Big brother can't have that, so something had to be done. So, in 1974, the U.S. Congress passed the Employee Retirement Income Security Act (ERISA), which led to retirement vehicles like the 401(k).[30]

This forced millions of workers who had an employer-provided pension plans to put all their retirement money in the stock market and mutual funds via a 401k—giving Wall Street control of the money. It was better for the company because it no longer had to pay those workers a paycheck for life via a pension plan. It was a primary catalyst for pushing the baby boomers' retirement money and into the stock market, causing a boom in the 70s.[31]

But then, what's going to happen to the stock market when the baby boomers start retiring and drawing on that money? They'll start selling, not buying, and when people sell more than buying, the stock market goes down.

So, what's the problem with the 401(k) if investing in the stock market is good? Many funds we get to choose from are on the list only because the fund company paid the provider to include them. These funds are actively managed, so they're expensive.

> Be fearful when others are greedy. Be greedy when others are fearful.
> —Warren Buffett

And they're rarely the best performers. In some cases, they even charge a front-end load fee that often amounts to 3% of our assets to buy the fund in the first place.[32]

If we work for a smaller company, the chances are we'll be forced to invest in the funds with higher fees. We should control our money and not have someone else do it. Some employers will match what you put in, if this is the case, take full advantage. Put in whatever the company will match and nothing more. It's free money after all.

Financial Advisor or Not?

There are a lot of so-called financial advisors and professional stock managers. Trying to pick one can be daunting. When it comes to "professional portfolio managers," just say no. Remember when I said that mutual funds have "professionals," but they do more harm than good? There was a quick study done in 2012 to see how good a professional would do with an amateur. This amateur was a cat who'd throw a toy mouse over a grid of companies. For a year, his picks yielded 11% in returns vs. the professional with 3% in returns.

As you can see, we have the same chances of doing it ourselves and saving the fees as we hire a pro. If we so deem to get one, it's best to get a fiduciary one by asking if they're fiduciary or not. A fiduciary is an investment professional, and they're legally required to put clients' interests ahead of their own, versus only recommending what'll result in a higher commission for themselves.

For more information, I recommend Tony Robbins book, *Unshakable*.

Remember, when it comes to fees, even 2% can mean a huge difference. Remember compound interest? Well, it works both ways. Those fees can result in thousands, if not millions of dollars. Let's say we have a retirement fund that earns 7% and charges us a 2% annual fee.

Over fifty years, that difference would have cost us 2/3rds (63%) of what we would have had.

IRA and Roth IRA

An individual retirement account (IRA) allows us to save money for retirement and as of 2020 it has a max contribution of $6,000 per year and earns interest roughly at around 6-8% but with tax-free growth. Just keep in mind that you will need to tell your Roth IRA what to invest in. If you don't, it will just be like a bank and hold your money with no growth. I would recommend filling it up with Index Funds of your choosing.

Some of us may wonder what the difference is between a traditional IRA and a Roth IRA, but there's only one significant difference between them, and that's how and when we get a tax break.

With a traditional IRA, our contributions are tax-deductible in the year they're made. So, when we make our investment we're taxed according to that year. As for a Roth IRA, we're taxed before our investment, so our withdrawals in retirement aren't taxed. This is all dependent on whether we think we'll be taxed more now or in the future. Which one to invest in depends on when we want to get taxed, either that current year or when we withdraw.

Annuities

There are two kinds of annuities—fixed and variable. There's no need to discuss this one in detail since fixed is a terrible idea. They work in the same manner as a savings account, but they are held with an insurance company and usually pay around 5% return. But as we learned previously, we need to have, at the very least, a 7% rate of return. A variable annuity one works with mutual funds, and they guarantee our principle. If we invest $100k and the value of the fund drops, we'll still keep our $100k. That may seem like a fail-safe, but remember our Risk-Return Ratio—the less risk, the lower the return, so these are typically better the closer we are to retirement.

Life Insurance

Just typing these two words makes my eyes glaze over. Insurance is one of those things we hate to pay for, but when something happens, if it ever does, we're glad we did. There are different types of life insurance:

> **Variable Life Insurance:** a permanent life insurance product with separate accounts comprised of various instruments and investment funds, such as stocks, bonds, equity funds, money market funds, and bond funds.[33]

> **Term Life Insurance:** a type of life insurance that guarantees payment of a stated death benefit if the covered person dies during a specified term. Once the term expires, the policyholder can either renew it for another term, convert the policy to permanent coverage, or allow the policy to terminate.[34]

> **Whole Life Insurance:** provides coverage for the life of the insured. In addition to paying a death benefit, whole life insurance also contains a savings component in which cash value may accumulate.[35]

> **Universal Life Insurance:** Universal life (UL) insurance is permanent life insurance with an investment savings element and low premiums similar to those of term life insurance.

> **Indexed Universal Life Insurance (IUL):** investment via stock market with life insurance protection.

I'm not going to go over each one of them. It's boring and can get a bit complicated. In order to make things simpler I would like to just say I like Indexed Universal Life Insurance or IUL Insurance because the policyholder can hold up to 100% of the policy's cash value to a stock market index, such as the S&P 500 or Nasdaq 100. If the indexed account increases, it gets added to the cash value of the policy, and it's all about those gains.

The upside is, it goes with the market and maintains a floor. This means if the market goes up, so does the cash value, but if the market drops, the existing cash value is protected from losses. On top of that, the cash value that accumulates is tax-deferred, the death benefit for beneficiaries and the loans made against the policy are tax free. There are also guaranteed premiums, death benefits, and provisions for long-term care and critical illness with different policies, so be sure to shop around.

There are some downsides like everything else, such as limited interest caps, which means if we have a year like 2019 with a 30.43% return, we capped at what the policy dictates, normally about 10-12%. The rate of return favors the company that sells the policy. IUL also has a greater risk, but mainly because it's tied to the market fluctuations.

There are also many fees and costs associated with them and can be expensive and can get complicated when getting a pricing structure. An IUL policy is like getting the best of both worlds. Not only do we get death benefits, but we also get a fixed contract without being directly invested in the market. Since we are capped we can enjoy some of the market booms gains, but we will be protected from major crashes.

Niefeld says, "The ideal customer is an individual who wants/needs life insurance, does not have the risk tolerance for a variable product, [but] would take some risk [in order] to receive a crediting rate higher than a fixed rate of return."[36]

My best suggestion for determining which to go with is what's the best fit for us. Take time to find out more of each and go with the one that suits us best. I like IUL because it's also an investment, but if we're older, we may want to choose something more secure. Life insurance is important, so be sure to get one that fits best and not what someone else recommends.

Real Estate!

When we talk about investing, we can't avoid talking about real estate. As Mark Twain says, "Buy land. They are not making it anymore." And with good reason too. It's one of the best investments we can make, but it does require a lot of capital. With everything, it's something where we need to do research. It may be a good investment, but that doesn't mean that it can't go wrong. Ask anyone who went through the 2009 housing crisis.

Any book by Dave Ramsey will advise us not to buy real estate until we're entirely out of debt and not to borrow money to get real estate. While I agree that it's best when we don't have debt, I don't agree with not borrowing for the investment; it'll take a long time to save $200k so we can invest in a single house, and that's a single investment.

What Others Say

Influential people who don't agree with Dave Ramsey:

Robert Kiyosaki: "Use debt to become rich."

Grant Cardone: "Don't pay cash for your apartments. The debt used to buy apartments is good debt and should be used over and over again. Debt paid down by others is like a gift from God."

Ken McElroy: "Large investment property loans are secured by the assets themselves."

Brandon Turner: "All you need is leverage and with real estate, leverage usually comes in the form of a loan."

Brian Murray: "The more you borrow, the more leveraged you are."

Proverbs 31:16 tells us "She goes to inspect a field and buys it; with her earnings, she plants a vineyard."

What to Keep in Mind

There are several things we need to keep in mind when it comes to investing in any of these vehicles. First, we need to start saving now. We can't wait until we're older or when we have more money. As the old Chinese proverb goes, investing is a lot like planting a tree. The best time to plant one was twenty years ago, and the second-best time is today. Once we're out of debt, we can start investing. Second, start by investing in low-cost index funds. These match the market, and as we talked about earlier, even after all the crashes, the average return held still at 11%.

Don't go with a professional manager and only get a fiduciary advisor. We don't want to have someone recommend where to put our money if it's solely in their interest. It's okay to be aggressive when we're still in our 20s or 30s, but we want to secure our investments as we get closer to retirement. This means we slowly move from stocks to bonds, which will allow us to go from aggressive to conservative, while still getting a return.

Make sure fees remain less than 1%, which will enable us to keep more of our money rather than paying so much in fees.

A Quick Recap on Investing

- 401(k)—If the employer matches it, max it out, but beware of the fees (if not 1% or less, don't do it). Otherwise, try to get out of it and invest elsewhere.
- Roth IRA—Max it out, but don't forget to tell it what to invest in

- Annuities—Only do variable annuities closer to retirement.
- Stocks/Bonds/Index and Mutual funds—low index funds. Slow, steady, and over time. Move to bonds closer to retirement. If you are going to do Mutual Funds, be sure to look at their track record and most importantly the fees, keep them under 1%. This is why I would recommend index funds over mutual funds.
- Real Estate—Don't wait to buy; buy and wait.
- And most importantly, as Charlie Munger said,

"I think when you're buying jewelry for the woman you love, financial considerations probably should not enter into it."

With all the investing possibilities available, it can get a bit overwhelming. Focus on one thing at a time and never put in more than we can afford. This isn't our saving grace; it can all go away one day to the next. We must put our trust in God first and foremost. Give generously and invest the rest.

* * *

In the next chapter, I'll show where all of our money is going and how to start to protect ourselves. If you're not wise like serpents, this is where the wolves will tear you up limb from limb.

Action Step 11

Start Investing!

Open up all appropriate accounts. Use this chapter to see which ones will work best for you. You will find links to all of the brokerage accounts that I use so you don't have to worry about looking for them.
- Start investing as soon, as often and as much as you can.
- Start building your portfolio even if it's a little bit at a time
- Make sure you have a Roth IRA
- Use this chapter as a guide to know where to start
- Most importantly.... DON'T STOP!

INVESTING ACCOUNTS

☐ **Brokerage Account** - Pick one from the chapter that will be best for you and start setting up your portfolio.

☐ **Roth IRA** - You can set this up with one of the brokerages you choose from or open up one just for this. Just open one up!

☐ **Life Insurance** - Decide what option works best for you from the chapter.

If you have a 401k or any other retirement through your employer find out if and how much they match it and use that as your max contribution.

If they do not match it, see if you can get out and put it towards a Roth IRA and Index funds, but if you are unable to get out, continue as is without contributing more and put towards a Roth IRA and Index Funds.

CHAPTER 21
THE KING'S TAXES

"Is it right to pay the imperial tax to Caesar or not? Should we pay or shouldn't we?" Then Jesus said to them, "Give back to Caesar what is Caesar's and to God what is God's."

—Mark 12:14-15,17

Ah, taxes, who doesn't want to learn about taxes?! Don't worry, this won't be long and tedious; it might be one of the smallest chapters. But I want to point out that we all need to know about taxes and how to work with them instead of having them work against us.

Here's the thing, we all want a big income tax return. Did you know, however, that we aren't supposed to get a tax return? That's right! We shouldn't be getting a tax return, and we should be getting zero, nada, zilch.

Here's how it works. We work forty hours a week, and then on payday, the IRS comes in and says, "Hold up, I need my cut." By the way, they use our withholding number from when we began our job, so we're telling them how much to take.

They get their cut because they don't trust us to pay them on time, and then they give us what's left of *our* paycheck.

At the end of the year, we happily go into an H&R block or call up someone we know to do our taxes. Crossing your fingers, we find out we're going to get money back. The IRS is going, "Oops, we took too much; we'll return your taxes."

I'm going to have a side rant here. Don't be one of those people who say it's like forced savings. Have some self-control. If we want to, we should have that money automatically withdrawn and into a money market where we can earn interest.

Taxes are our most significant single expense. Someone already crunched these numbers, but it's estimated that we spend twenty-five to thirty-five percent of our lives working to pay taxes. That means that we're working for tax payments for more than two hours every day, three to four months of every year. That's thirteen years of our work life and twenty years of our lifetime. Talk about a twenty-year sentence.

In the early days, America was, for the most part, tax-free. It wasn't until 1862 that the first income tax was levied to pay for the Civil War. After that, in 1895, the U.S. Supreme Court ruled that an income tax was unconstitutional, but that didn't stop them. In 1913, the same year the Federal System was created, the 16th Amendment was passed, making income tax permanent. In the beginning, however, only the wealthy were taxed.[37]

We are probably all thinking it should have stayed like that. But then how would the government have control over our pockets? (That was a little bit of sarcasm.) It didn't occur to them until 1945 after WWII. The government found it to be a handy revenue-raising tool they could use to rebuild after the war, so they had to get more people involved. And so, they began taxing the middle class.

Then, something miraculous happened. As they tinkered with that tax code and watched, they saw a profound effect. The codes they put in place started to affect the economy. If they placed specific laws and codes to enforce taxes or deductions, the economy would follow suit.

To sway it to their liking, all they had to do was write a tax code for it. Here's the funny thing though, we may think we have no choice in the matter and have to pay taxes. That's where we're wrong! Tom Wheelwright writes, "Millions of people pay little to no taxes; the only difference between them and us is they understand how the tax law works. The tax law is a tool the government uses to shape the economy and promote social, agricultural, and energy policy, and it was made by the wealthy for the wealthy."

However, we don't need to be wealthy to take advantage of the codes. It's there for us too. Ever wonder why it is so long and boring? The wealthy made it like that for a reason. They know people won't read it on their off-time to learn the tax codes. That's all it'd take! In general, do the activities the government wants us to do and take advantage of the same codes!

I'm not a tax consultant, CPA, or accountant; anything in this chapter regarding deductions is a general term. To abide by the actual codes and work within them, we'll need to hire a professional. This is informational, so we can open our eyes and see we're sheep amid wolves, but we can be wise and follow the law.

We simply need to understand that the tax code is written for the rich; they write it so they can get incentives depending on what they want to do. They write it in a way so it's boring for us and so they never have to pay taxes or pay the minimum. They use this to their advantage so they can ultimately keep more of their money and gain prosperity. And that's why some people get mad; all they see is the rich aren't getting taxed enough. But they are! They know how to work the system, so they don't pay like the next person!

Let's take billionaire Warren Buffett. He pays less in taxes than we do, but don't hate because he does this by something called long-term capital gains tax. This tax is paid when we receive qualifying dividends, stocks, real estate, and most assets for more than a year. And the maximum you can be taxed on those things is 20% when you make $400,000 plus and with no cap on income.

Verses an employee that receives a W-2 and gets taxes a lot more and is totally dependent on income. Just look at the table below.

Rate	For Single Individuals, Taxable Income Over	For Married Individuals Filing Joint Returns, Taxable Income Over	For Heads of Households, Taxable Income Over
10%	$0	$0	$0
12%	$9,875	$19,750	$14,100
22%	$40,125	$80,250	$53,700
24%	$85,525	$171,050	$85,500
32%	$163,300	$326,600	$163,300
35%	$207,350	$414,700	$207,350
37%	$518,400	$622,050	$518,400

Source: Internal Revenue Service

The chart shows the current tax bracket, and as we can see a regular W-2 employee will get taxed above 20% as soon as they make over $40,000. This is why investing is so critical, because our investments are more valuable and are taxed a lot less than the money we make from a job.

But, here's the thing. We're taxed the same way the rich are. You, me, and every citizen, we're *all* governed by the same

> It's not how much you make that counts, but how much money you keep.
> —Robert Kiyosaki

tax code. So, any of us can take advantage of it. At the very surface level of things, the government wants the economy to grow.[38] They want us to invest in one of these areas:

Local Energy Production—That's why we get a tax break if we purchase solar panels for our home.

Local Agricultural—If we own land and have cattle, we probably already know the tax benefits you gain from this.

Economic Activities—Include investing into the market and the making, purchasing, and selling of goods and services. This would be an entrepreneur or businessperson.

Provide Housing—We should know that having apartments, building houses, or anything that provides housing has huge tax benefits.

Provide Employment—Simply having a business where we employ the community is a benefit.

Beyond that, if we have any of the above or start something that'll help us to take advantage of the tax codes, remember we need to make our expenses count. We need to make them work for us.

This is an over simplified explanation so that we can be aware that there are ways to decrease our taxes. When they work for us, they become necessary. And when our expenses are necessary, boom, they're a deductible.

The U.S. tax law calls this *a business purpose for our expenses*. I'm sure most of us have heard someone say, "I need my receipts to write them off, or it's a business expense." Some put their charitable contributions on their tax return. Do you know why? It's to minimize what they're getting taxed on. It's deducted from their income! To drive the point home, this is what the rich and wealthy do. We need to stop being so angry they're rich and say they should pay more in taxes. Stop with the finger-pointing. Learn some tax laws, and we, too, can take advantage. We're mad at the rich because they picked up a book, but we can read the same book.

Matthew 25:29 (NLT) tells us, "For to everyone who has, more will be given, and he will have abundance; but from him who does not have, even what he has will be taken away." I hope this chapter helped in our understanding of a lot of the truth about taxes. It's written for us to be able to take advantage of them. As I said before, I'm not a CPA or an accountant, and any further information can be found in many great books I recommend in the back of this book. Learn the tax laws, and we can get wealthy simply by following the rules.

I also recommend if we're going to start a business, we should first sit down with a CPA to see which is best for us. Whether it's sole proprietor, LLC, S-Corp, or C-Corp, they all have benefits; some have more tax-deferred options and protections.

In A Nutshell

When we're employed, the process goes like this:
- We work for our income.
- The IRS takes its cut.
- We get the rest to pay for our expenses.

When we have a business, the process is a little different:
- We bring in income via sales or service.
- We pay for our expenses.
- We pay the IRS taxes on whatever is left.

In the end, we tell the IRS what to tax us on instead of taxing us on everything we worked for.

Again, I'm not a CPA or an accountant, so when we start a business, we should hire a professional and do our due diligence. We can save ourselves a lot of money by being in the know and working within the tax code instead of against it.

* * *

The last thing I want to discuss in this book is teaching our children all we've learned in a way they can understand. The next chapter gives some guidelines so we can teach what they won't learn in school.

CHAPTER 22
INSTRUCT THEM DAY AND NIGHT

A good man leaves an inheritance
to his children's children.

—Proverbs 13:22 NKJV

The very last thing we need to cover is teaching our children and our children's children. As we discussed, the schools aren't going to teach our children about finances and how money works. This is all up to us.

We need to leave an inheritance to them so they can continue with their families. An inheritance isn't limited to money. It also includes Godly character qualities like integrity and trustworthiness. Combining a financial inheritance with wisdom and Godliness ensures the next generation will also manage God's blessings God's way for God's glory, long after we've graduated to heaven.[39]

A man, as the head and spiritual leader, needs to educate the household. How important is it for the man to teach his family?

- Genesis 2:15-17 tells us, "The Lord God placed the man in the Garden of Eden to tend and watch over it. But the Lord God warned him, 'You may freely eat the fruit of every tree in the garden except the tree of the knowledge of good and evil. If you eat its fruit, you are sure to die.'"
- Genesis 2:19 tells us, "So the Lord God formed from the ground all the wild animals and all the birds of the sky."
- Genesis 2:22 tells us, "Then the Lord God made a woman from the rib, and he brought her to the man."

Genesis 3 The Fall

As you can see, God gave Adam instructions about the forbidden fruit, and then He created Eve. It was Adam's obligation to show Eve the law that was given to him. She was aware, but we can't tell someone and then leave them to their own. We need to instruct, show, and make an example of what's expected. When it comes to our children, it's no different.

Is there any question why these verses are back-to-back? We're to direct our children on the right path, and one of the main things is being wise with our finances. Before you can teach how to manage money, we first need to manage ours. We need to model behavior before we can expect them to follow us, just as Jesus came and was a model for us. 1 Corinthians 11:1 tells us, "Follow my example, as I follow the example of Christ."

> Direct your children onto the right path, and when they are older, they will not leave it. Just as the rich rule, the poor, so the borrower is servant to the lender.
> —Proverbs 22:6-7 (NLT)

Once we begin to model the behavior we want, we need to explain it to them verbally. Deuteronomy 6:7 (NKJV) tells us, "You shall teach them diligently to your children, and shall talk of them when you sit in your house, when you walk by the way, when you lie down, and when you rise up."

By the time our children are five years old, it's best to start them off with earning a small income. Whether it's earned or an allowance, the amount should be decided by the parents and child's ability. But as soon as they're old enough to understand, they should know Money=Work.

However, I need to make this point. There's a difference between working for money and chores. Children need to understand that there are individual work requirements we don't get paid for but are expected to do. We don't get paid to clean our house. They shouldn't expect to get paid for chores. These responsibilities are necessary as they get older and have a home; no one will be paying them. For added duties, they can get a set pay.

Let them learn that there are consequences when they make mistakes, and don't bail them out. Establish boundaries and advice but let them have freedom of choice. Above all, teach budgeting as their age permits. These rules aren't set in stone; it all depends on the maturity of the child.

At each age group, we can teach them something and then add as they get older. From ages three to five, they can understand the concept of working and getting an instant reward. With that reward, they can learn to give and save for purchases. This is the best time to teach a child to give from that which they've earned. I'd recommend having that as the highlight of their reward.

By the time they're six, they can understand bigger concepts, and up until the age of twelve, we can start teaching them budgeting on a small scale, which will include giving, saving, and spending. Their savings can be for bigger purchases, and they can now spend on little things they want. After, they can start working for money.

THEY NEED TO KNOW HOW TO:

Give: Start with tithing

Save: Pay yourself first & for emergencies ONLY

Invest: Short & Long term

Spend: Diff. Needs & Wants

Remember, there's a difference between chores and working on top of that for cash.

Once they're the age of twelve, they're old enough to be exposed to the family budget and what's going on behind the scenes. Eventually as they start understanding more they should start being involved in the family budgeting, and we can start teaching them skills such as shopping, ability to distinguish needs from wants, paying bills, saving and investing, and waiting for the Lord to provide. Showing them how to give, save, and spend will give them a good foundation to succeed in managing their finances.

Another thing to show them is how to distinguish good from bad debt. We can show them this by letting our children borrow money from us and pay us back with interest while calculating how much they spent.

For good debt, he/she can borrow money that will get a return. For example, purchasing a lawnmower on credit (Dad's Bank) and then mowing lawns to generate income to pay the lawnmower off with that income while having some cash flow.

Ages Matter

AGES 3-5	AGES 6-12	AGES 13-18
Teach Work-Reward	Work For Money	In Depth Budgeting
Instant Payout	Budgeting	Investing
Teach How to Give	Amount is Up to You	Planning Ahead
Save to Spend	Give, Save, Spend	Debt

One of the most important things I've learned is we need to stop playing with our kids so much and start working with them. Sure, playing with them is fun and enjoyable at times, but they will learn more and remember more from what we taught them while working.

CONCLUSION

I hope we can know the simplicity of what we can accomplish if we follow the principles outlined here. Sure, there will be stress, struggles, and some resistance, but we'll come out ahead so long as we stick through it. All of this takes time. Anything worth it will take time and determination. All we need to do is start with a concentrated effort to make our futures easier.

A lot of people say it's a lot of work and takes too long. These are the same people who are working a job for forty years only to have enough income during retirement—*maybe*. Some even have to work part-time after retirement. Isn't that time frame much longer than putting in the effort now?

Work needs to be deliberate; stop wasting time!

According to Seneca, "People are frugal in guarding their personal property or their money; but as soon as it comes to squandering time, they are most wasteful of the one thing in which it is right to be stingy."

We miss the most important instruction of all. We all know it. Genesis 1:28 says, "God blessed them and said to them, "Be fruitful and multiply; fill the earth and subdue it. Rule and have dominion over the fish in the sea and the birds in the sky and over every living creature that moves on the ground."

1. Be fruitful.
2. Multiply, fill, and subdue
3. Rule and have dominion.

And most of us simply *be*, we never do but still want to have and wonder why we don't.

It's simple physics.

To have power, we need to do the work over a certain amount of time. We have already done the physical formula.

$$P=W/t$$

Energy is neither created nor destroyed, but it's transferable. But we can't get high energy from a low energy source.

To have high power, we need to do more work, fill more, and subdue more over a certain amount of time. We can't have more if we don't do more.

Be fruitful in your time. Do fill, do subdue, and do multiply all work overtime on earth so that we can have power, rule, and dominion.

And with that same equation, we can all agree, putting in more time with less work doesn't give us more power. Doing nothing, day in day out, waiting to get paid, and waiting for vacay doesn't give us more power.

But we also see how there's more to do to have more. If we increase the work over time, we get more power. We need to stop wasting time and start doing more so we can have more.

I wanted to bring up one last key important point that it's not our money.

> It is not that we have a short time to live, but that we waste a lot of it. Life is long if we know how to use it.
> —Seneca

It was provided for and entrusted to us by our Lord and Savior. We need to save and be ready for retirement, but we can't depend on it. There is only one we need to depend on, and that's our creator.

The market may crash, it will most certainly fluctuate, and we can never predict it. But one thing for sure is our God will always be there. He's our primary source for everything. We need to save, but not hoard; we need to invest but not depend on it. There's a fine line that needs to be met. We're here to be good stewards with everything He's entrusted to us. But in the end, it's all His, and we'll be taken care of by Him.

Our main purpose here on Earth is to glorify and worship Him. There's a fine line when it comes to saving, investing, and spending. The Bible tells us in Proverbs 21:5 (NLT) to save for the future. "Good planning and hard work lead to prosperity, but hasty shortcuts lead to poverty."

Proverbs 6:6,8 also tells us, "Go to the ant, you sluggard; consider its ways and be wise!; it stores its provisions in summer and gathers its food at harvest." But then at the same time, it directs us not to hoard for ourselves as we read in Matthew 6:19. "Do not store up for yourselves treasures on earth, where moths and vermin destroy, and where thieves break in and steal."

It's not a contradiction in any way. There's a difference with being wise with what we have and another to think we can store it all up, and it'll be our saving grace. We see we're to store up treasures in heaven. Ultimately, with this book, that's what I want us to do. I want us to live a financially free life and make wealth for ourselves, our families, and our children's children. But along the way, I want us to be blessed more than we can imagine so we can be a blessing to others.

We can't help someone out of a hole if we're standing right next to them. As previously stated, money is a tool, and we can use it for wonderous things. We need to take it off its pedestal and recognize we're the master of it. The power it has is the one we give it. It's nothing, and it's fleeting. We can make it; we can use it, and we can help with it. We don't need to hoard it with a white-knuckle grasp. Money does come and go, and there's more than enough of it to go around.

I've shown how to get out of debt, budget, and build wealth. All that is great, and God isn't telling us not to do it. He's telling us that it won't save us, and we definitely can't take it with us. But while we have it, we can help and love our neighbors. I ask we all stay blessed and be a blessing to others. Give and give generously.

Command those who are rich in this present world not to be arrogant nor to put their hope in wealth, which is so uncertain, but to put their hope in God, who richly provides us with everything for our enjoyment. Command them to do good, to be rich in good deeds, and to be

generous and willing to share. In this way, they
will lay up treasure for themselves as a firm
foundation for the coming age, so that they may
take hold of the life that is truly life.

—1 Timothy 6:17-19

This book may have gone against the grain in some
parts, but in the end, I want us to open our eyes and
hearts. We're fed a bunch of lies; we're told one thing
and believed it. There's more out there, and we need to
know about it. We're merely sheep amid wolves, and we
need to be wise as serpents and learn and find out for
ourselves so we can be as innocent as doves by working
within the law.

We have enough poor people in the world; we need
wealthy followers of God to overthrow Satan's dominion on this Earth. We can stand together and make a
massive change! Stay blessed my brothers and sisters,
so when that day comes, you can hear . . .

"Well done good and faithful servants."

I send you out as sheep amid wolves. Therefore, be wise as serpents and innocent as doves.

—Matthew 10:16

ENDNOTES

Ancillary 1 — End Notes

1 "Poverty Guidelines." U.S. Department of Health & Human Services, March 5, 2020. https://aspe.hhs.gov/poverty-guidelines.

2 *G. Edward Griffin in The Creature from Jekyll Island, on Rockefeller's General Education Board, founded in 1903*

3 Anderson, Peter. "10 Bible Verses About Contentment: How Can We Feel Contentment In A Restless World?," February 19, 2020. https://www.biblemoneymatters.com/10-bible-verses-about-contentment-how-can-we-feel-contentment-in-a-restless-world/.

4 Dispenza, Joe. *Breaking the Habit of Being Yourself: How to Lose Your Mind and Create a New One.* Carlsbad, CA: Hay House, 2016.

5 Berg, Yehuda. "The Power of Words," November 17, 2011. https://www.huffpost.com/entry/the-power-of-words_1_b_716183.

6   Sikora, Joanna, M.D.R. Evans, and Jonathan Kelley. "Scholarly Culture: How Books in Adolescence Enhance Adult Literacy, Numeracy and Technology Skills in 31 Societies," October 2, 2018. https://www.sciencedirect.com/science/article/abs/pii/S0049089X18300607.

7   Louder, Bob. "First Things First." Christian Financial Ministries, 2019. http://christianfinancialministries.org/first-things-first/.

8   Sehgal, Kabir. *Coined: the Rich Life of Money and How Its History Has Shaped Us*. New York, NY: Grand Central Publishing, 2015.

9   *G. Edward Griffin in The Creature from Jekyll Island, on Rockefeller's General Education Board, founded in 1903*

10   Grabmeier, Jeff. "70 Percent of College Students Stressed about Finances." Ohio State News, July 12, 2018. https://news.osu.edu/70-percent-of-college-students-stressed-about-finances/.

11   Roeder, Phil. Data USA, 2018. https://datausa.io/profile/geo/washington-dc/.

12   Bethune, Sophie. "Money Stress Weighs on Americans' Health." Monitor on Psychology. American Psychological Association, April 2015. https://www.apa.org/monitor/2015/04/money-stress.

13   Friedman, Zack. "78% Of Workers Live Paycheck To Paycheck." Forbes. Forbes Magazine, January 11, 2019. https://www.forbes.com/sites/zackfriedman/2019/01/11/live-paycheck-to-paycheck-government-shutdown/.

14   Gainer, Michael. "Facts on Homelessness," October 5, 2020. https://www.projecthome.org/about/facts-homelessness.

15   Morris, Robert. *Beyond Blessed: God's Perfect Plan to Overcome All Financial Stress*. Nashville, TN: Faith Words, 2019.

16   MacDonald, Jay, and Taylor Tompkins. "The History of Credit Cards (Timeline & Major Events)." CreditCards.

com, November 3, 2020. https://www.creditcards.com/
credit-card-news/history-of-credit-cards.php.

17 Steele, Jason. "The History of Credit Cards." Experian.
Experian, January 21, 2020. https://www.experian.com/
blogs/ask-experian/the-history-of-credit-cards/.

18 Fay, Bill. "The U.S. Consumer Debt Crisis." Debt.
org, November 7, 2019. https://www.debt.org/faqs/
americans-in-debt/.

19 Skowronski, Jeanine. "Lesson #26 : 15 Surprising
Things That Affect Your Credit Score." Credit
Warriors, November 3, 2020. https://www.creditwar-
riors.org/15-surprising-things-affect-credit-score/.

20 Rathner, Sara, and NerdWallet's Credit Card
Expert. "NerdWallet's 2019 Household Debt Study."
NerdWallet, 2019. https://www.nerdwallet.com/blog/
average-credit-card-debt-household/.

21 Dayton, Howard. *Your Money Counts: the Biblical Guide to
Earning, Spending, Saving, Investing, Giving, and Getting
out of Debt.* Carol Stream, IL: Tyndale House Publishers,
2011.

22 Sweet, Joni. "What Is a Trigger Lead and Is It Legal?"
LendingTree, 2019. https://www.lendingtree.com/
credit-repair/what-is-a-trigger-lead/.

23 "Current US Inflation Rates: 2009-2020." US Inflation
Calculator, October 13, 2020. https://www.usinflation-
calculator.com/inflation/current-inflation-rates/.

24 Kiersz, Andy. "Actually, Young People SHOULD Invest
in Their 401(k) Plans ..." Business Insider. Business
Insider, April 22, 2015. https://www.businessinsider.
com/compound-interest-and-young-people-2015-4.

25 Leonhardt, Megan. "If You Invested $1,000 in
Amazon in 1997, Here's How Much You'd Have
Now." CNBC. CNBC, August 31, 2018. https://www.
cnbc.com/2018/08/31/if-you-put-1000-dollars-i

n-amazon-in-1997-heres-how-much-youd-have-now.
html.

26   Broker, AM. "Learn Stocks for Beginners: How to Start, How to Succeed," October 12, 2020. https://www.ambroker.com/en/analysis/blog/learn-stocks-beginners/.

27   Kennon, Joshua. "How to Invest In Stocks." The Balance, 2020. https://www.thebalance.com/stocks-4073971.

28   Waggoner, John. "The 25 Best Mutual Funds of All Time." Kiplinger. Kiplinger, October 21, 2019. https://www.kiplinger.com/slideshow/investing/t041-s001-the-25-best-mutual-funds-of-all-time/index.html.

29

30   Miller, Rebecca J. "ERISA: 40 Years Later," September 1, 2014. https://www.journalofaccountancy.com/issues/2014/sep/erisa-20149881.html.

31   Kiyosaki, Robert T. *Rich Dad's Conspiracy of the Rich: the 8 New Rules of Money*. New York, NY: Business Plus, 2009.

32   Robbins, Anthony, and Peter Mallouk. *Unshakeable: Your Financial Freedom Playbook*. New York, NY: Simon & Schuster, 2017.

33   Kagan, Julia. "Variable Life Insurance." Investopedia. Investopedia, September 24, 2020. https://www.investopedia.com/terms/v/variablelifeinsurancepolicy.asp.

34   "Life Insurance." Genesis Life Group, 2020. https://www.burialinsurancenc.com/lifeinsurance.

35   Kagan, Julia. "What Is Whole Life Insurance?" Investopedia. Investopedia, September 23, 2020. https://www.investopedia.com/terms/w/wholelife.asp.

36   Rotter, Kimberly. "Indexed Universal Life Insurance: The Pros & Cons." Investopedia. Investopedia, September 23, 2020. https://www.investopedia.com/articles/personal-finance/070215/pros-cons-indexed-universal-life-insurance.asp.

37 Terrell, Ellen. "History of the US Income Tax." History of the US Income Tax (Business Reference Services, Library of Congress), 2004. https://www.loc.gov/rr/business/hottopic/irs_history.html.

38 Wheelwright, Tom. *Tax-Free Wealth: How to Build Massive Wealth by Permanently Lowering Your Taxes.* Scottsdale, AZ: RDA Press, 2015.

39 Ramsey Solutions, Dave. "3 Bible Verses That Will Help You Leave a Legacy." daveramsey.com. Ramsey Solutions, October 15, 2019. https://www.daveramsey.com/blog/3-bible-verses-legacy.

Ancillary 2 – Forms

Get the download or excel versions by going to www.
sheepamidwolves.com/forms

You can use the Excel sheets to auto calculate after
putting in your information.

1. Calculate Cashflow
2. Calculate Net Worth
3. Command Your Money – Getting to Zero
4. Debt Management Payoff
5. Investing Management

Take the Finanical IQ Assesment Survey!

You can find out where you stand by taking our Financial
IQ Assesment. Quickly understand where you are at in
your Finanical IQ and get insights of other bonuses for
your next steps to gain financial freedom.

Visit sheepamidwolves.com/financial-assesment

CALCULATE CASH FLOW

	Income 1	
INCOME (Insert total monthly income)	Extra income	
	Total monthly income	
	Expenses (Add up all totals minus loans)	
EXPENSES	Debt (Add loans total)	
	Total monthly expenses	
CASH FLOW	**Total Income - Total Expenses**	

HOUSING	Actual Cost
Mortgage or rent	
Phone	
Electricity	
Gas	
Water and sewer	
Cable	
Waste removal	
Maintenance or repairs	
Supplies	
Other	
Total	

TRANSPORTATION	Actual Cost
Vehicle payment	
Bus/taxi fare	
Insurance	
Licensing	
Fuel	
Maintenance	
Other	
Total	

INSURANCE	Actual Cost
Home	
Health	
Life	
Other	
Total	

FOOD	Actual Cost
Groceries	
Dining out	
Other	
Total	

ENTERTAINMENT	Actual Cost
Video/DVD	
CDs	
Movies	
Concerts	
Sporting events	
Live theater	
Other	
Other	
Other	
Total	

LOANS	Actual Cost
Personal	
Student	
Credit card	
Credit card	
Credit card	
Other	
Total	

PERSONAL CARE	Actual Cost
Medical	
Hair/nails	
Clothing	
Dry cleaning	
Health club	
Organization dues or fees	
Other	
Total	

PETS	Actual Cost
Food	
Medical	
Grooming	
Toys	
Other	
Total	

CALCULATE NET WORTH

ASSETS	Annual Cash Flow (Cash Flow X 12)	
	Total ofAssets	
	Total Assets	
LIABILITIES	Liabilites (Add liabilities minus Credit Cards)	
	Credit Card (Add all Credit Cards)	
	Total Liabilities	
EQUITY/NET WORTH	**Total Assets - Total Liabilities**	

ASSETS	VALUE		LIABILITIES	TOTAL OWED
Paid Off Home			Mortgage	
Paid Off Vehicle 1			Vehicle Loan 1	
Paid Off Vehicle 2			Vehicle Loan 2	
Gold/Silver/Precious Metals/Stone			Personal Loans	
Retirement Accounts			Student Loans	
IRA/Roth IRAs			Other	
401k			Credit card 1	
Stocks/Bonds/Mutual Funds			Credit card 2	
Supplies			Credit card 3	
Other			Credit card 4	
Total			Total	

Debt Mangement Pay Off

Total Monthy Payments	
Extra Cash flow	
Available Towards Frist Pay Off - Total Debt Payments)	(Extra Cash Flow

LIABILITIES	TOTAL OWED	MINIMUM PAYMENT
Totals		

List from liabilities chart from smallest amount to largest NOT including mortgage

COMMAND YOUR MONEY

INCOME	Income 1	
	Extra income	
	Total monthly income	
EXPENSES	Expenses	
	Towards Debt/Investing/Savings	
	Total monthly expenses	
GET TO ZERO	Subtract Total Expenses from Total Income to get zero (Make adjustments where necessary)	

HOUSING	Amount
Tithe	
Rent/Mortgage	
Electricity	
Gas	
Water and sewer	
Cable	
Phone	
Maintenance or repairs	
Supplies	
Other	
Total	

FOOD	Amount
Groceries	
Other	
Total	

INSURANCE	Amount
Home	
Health	
Life	
Other	
Total	

TRANSPORTATION	Amount
Vehicle payment	
Bus/taxi fare	
Insurance	
Licensing	
Fuel	
Maintenance	
Other	
Total	

ENTERTAINMENT	Amount
Dining Out	
Hobbies	
Movies	
Concerts	
Sporting events	
Other	
Total	

Investing & Savings	Amount
Self Investing	
Roth IRA	
Stock Portfolio	
Index Funds/Other	
Business Venture	
Savings	
Other	
Total	

LOANS	Amount
Personal	
Student	
Credit card 1	
Credit card 2	
Other	
Total	

PERSONAL CARE	Amount
Medical	
Hair/nails	
Clothing	
Dry cleaning	
Health club	
Other	
Total	

PETS	Amount
Food	
Medical	
Grooming	
Toys	
Other	
Total	

Minimum Percentages	Actual
Tithe (10%)	
Living Expenses (50%)	
Investing & Savings (20%)	
Entertainment (20%)	
To find you actual percentages take the total of each and divide it by your total income. (Total Amount / Total Income) X 100	

LONG TERM INVESTING

Date	Ticker	# of shares	Entry Price	Total Amount	Notes

Ancillary 3 – Book Recommendations

For more recommendations visit www.thebiblicalentrepreneur.com/best-books

THE RICHEST MAN IN BABYLON

https://amzn.to/3orIjty

CRYPTOASSETS

https://amzn.to/3kwGqth

BREAKING THE HABIT OF BEING YOURSELF

https://amzn.to/31Ejb96

THE CREATURE FROM JEKYLL ISLAND

https://amzn.to/34pxAIi

TAX FREE WEALTH

https://amzn.to/35BwyIm

MONEY MASTER THE GAME

https://amzn.to/3mjPvpR

THINK AND GROW RICH

https://amzn.to/35z1vx2

RICH DAD POOR DAD

https://amzn.to/3juCJms

Ancillary 4 – Brokerage Accounts

Visit sheepamidwolves.com/investing for each of the mobile apps or use the QR Code.

ACORNS
https://bit.ly/invest-acorns

M1 FINANCE
https://bit.ly/invest-m1

CHARLES SCHWAB
http://bit.ly/invest-schwab

E-TRADE
http://bit.ly/invest-etrade

TD AMERITRADE
https://bit.ly/invest-tdts

ROBINHOOD
https://bit.ly/invest-robinhood

PUBLIC
https://bit.ly/invest-public

WEBULL
https://bit.ly/invest-webull

TASTYWORKS
https://bit.ly/invest-tastyworks

ALLY INVEST
http://bit.ly/invest-ally

FIDELITY
http://bit.ly/invest-fidelity

INTERACTIVE
http://bit.ly/invest-interactive

Ancillary 5 – End of Chapter Questions

Chapter 1

1. What are things that you can think of that have stopped you from making more income?
2. Are there factors in your life that still hold you back?
3. When the Bible is mentioned to you, what feelings does it bring up?
4. What has been your thinking about how to make more money?

Chapter 2

1. What are false beliefs that you grew up with?
2. What are things that you are thankful for?
3. What do you have trouble being content with?
4. Is being thankful, content or both difficult at times? When are some of those times?

Chapter 3

1. Do you curse regularly? How can you make a conscious decision to stop cursing?
2. What are other words that you say that may be cursing you?
3. Are there phrases that you need to change from your speech?
4. What are some replacement phrases that you can add to your vocabulary that you can start using right away?

Chapter 4

1. What was your first interpretation of the parable of the rich man and the camel through the eye of the needle?
2. Are there certain things in your life that you are putting ahead of Christ?
3. If Jesus was speaking to you, what would he ask you to give up for him?
4. What lesson did you take from this parable?

Chapter 5

1. What are the differences of character between the rich men of the Bible and yourself?
2. Which one can you identify yourself with the most? Strengths or weaknesses.
3. What can you do to be more like these great men?

Chapter 6

1. Did you ever see yourself as an image of God with the ability to create?
2. Is there moments where you have noticed you do not have high energy?
3. Have you ever worried about not being able to pay a bill or food? Does God's promise bring you comfort?
4. Do you find yourself being more trusting of God and his promises?

Chapter 7

1. Have you been deceived by only looking at the lack of things?
2. Where do you mainly see a lack of something in?
3. Can you change your perspective and see the abundance?
4. What other areas are being affected by having a not enough mentality?

Chapter 8

1. Are you comfortable with learning new things?
2. What are new things that you can learn to improve your overall skill set?
3. What five things are you willing to research about and start learning?
4. What are your current hobbies that you can become and an expert in and eventually monetize?

Chapter 9

1. What is something that you always wanted to know but would give up after several failed attempts?
2. What were you told as far as the American Dream?
3. Were you trying to accomplish this dream in your life?
4. How much do you really know about money?

Chapter 10

1. What are your thoughts when you think about money as a Christian?
2. Is it a topic that doesn't get discussed in your circle of friends? If so do you know why?
3. How has this chapter changed the way you think and will it affect how you speak about it?
4. What are things you can do so that you can start becoming more of a blessing?

Chapter 11

1) What did you think money was? Did you ever think about it?
2. Do you think of it different now that you know it's a note of debt? Do you have the same faith in it as before?
3. Where do you think our currency is headed next and the level of faith we have in it?
4. What are your thoughts on cryptocurrency.

Chapter 12

1. Do you think that money is good?
2. How do you feel about this chapter overall?
3. Can you recognize that it's a design in God's plan? If so, how?
4. Where do you feel in your life that it was a providence, possession and a provision?

Chapter 13

1. What are other good things that you can think about when it comes to money?
2. How do you feel about Mark Twain's quote "The lack of money is the root of all evil."?
3. Does knowing the bad side help you become better at controlling your money?
4. How does it make you feel to know that this is Satan's kingdom and he doesn't want Christians to have financial education or influence?

Chapter 14

1. What level are you currently on? Remember it's not about how much you make but how you handle what you have.
2. Can you see yourself becoming financially free now that you have a birds eye view? If not, what is prohibiting you?
3. Did you ever think it was as easy as just managing your money correctly?
4. What can you start doing today that will help you get started in becoming financially free?
5. After doing your cash flow and net worth, are you able to see what area you need help in?

Chapter 15

1. Do you consider yourself a good steward? If so, how? If not, what can you do to improve?

2. How many unnecessary monthly payments are you making?

3. What do you think will be the hardest step in the 9 steps to conquer?

4. Are you willing to make some sacrifices now to improve your future?

Chapter 16

1) Have you been tithing as much as you should have?

2. Do you have any concerns about giving tithe?

3. Will you be willing to commit to tithe first before bills and trust in the Lord?

4. What charities or movements are you passionate about and want to help with?

Chapter 17

1. Would you consider yourself a saver or a spender?

2. Are you close to your beginner emergency savings or are you at 3-6 months of savings? If not, what are some things you know you can do to get to that goal?

3. Are there any big purchases in your near future that you can start planning for now? Is it feasible?

4. What are other types of savings you can start for yourself?

Chapter 18

1. How faithful have you been with the amount you currently have? Is there more you can do?
2. Aside from the basic needs listed, are there others that have a priority in your life?
3. After listing all of you expenses, can you see how you can make some changes in order to have more or to get out of debt?
4. How confident do you feel about using the bank account method for budgeting?
5. How do you feel now that you are going to command you money versus budgeting?
6. Will you be able to make the sacrifices needed in order to be able to command your money better?

Chapter 19

1. How did you view debt before reading this book?
2. How has that changed since reading?
3. If you are in debt, have you committed to using the snowball method to free yourself from debt?
4. What are other methods that you have tried that didn't work and discouraged you from continuing?

Chapter 20

1. Do you currently have any type of investment or retirement accounts? If so, what type do you currently have?

2. What are some things that you can start doing to invest in yourself?

3. Are you familiar with how much you are paying in fees and how much your returns are?

4. Did this chapter give you any ideas on investing or other ways of bringing in more income?

5. How comfortable are you now regarding the knowledge of investments? Did this chapter give you a better understanding?

6. Will you be able to take that understanding and start investing even if it's a little to start?

Chapter 21

1. What are your thoughts now regarding taxes and income tax?

2. How has this chapter helped you understand how important it is to be aware of taxes and what you can do to minimize how much you pay?

3. Do you feel like you can start implementing one of these strategies to help you in your taxes?

4. How has this chapter opened your mind to the possibilities? Are you wanting to explore more into this subject to learn more?

5. Do you see the importance of hiring a good CPA?

Chapter 22

1. How important is it to you to leave an inheritance to your children?
2. Did you ever think of leaving one for your children's children?
3. Do you feel more confident now to instruct your children on finances?

Conclusion

1. Look back and examine how your mindset has changed regarding money and the Bible.
2. Do you feel confident in your knowledge for finances after reading this book?
3. Will you take the next steps and put what you learned to work so that you can be financially free?
4. Are you ready to become financially free?
5. What does that look like to you?
6. What are your goals when it comes to time, age and amount?

Ancillary 6 – Acknowledgements

First and foremost, praises and thanks to the God, the Almighty, for His showers of blessings and Holy Spirit's wisdom and guidance throughout the writing of this book. He is the reason the book has been written and is published. Nothing is accomplished without Him.

I would also like to thank my parents for their continued support and encouragement throughout my life. I am extremely grateful for their love, prayers, caring and sacrifices that they have had to endure, and I seek only to be able to repay them ten times fold. I am glad that I can now be able to show them the knowledge I have gathered over the years.

I want to thank Danny Veiga and Eddie Silva for their friendship and guidance. Both of them were the first friendships I developed in my entrepreneurial journey. They helped me break free from a lack mentality and shared their knowledge when I was first starting out. I couldn't have asked for better friends in the beginning of my ventures. They will always be a part of my life and an extension of my family. A shout out goes to Gallant Dill, one of my first official mentors. He showed me how to gain control of my life, and it was because of him that I finally got the courage to burn the boats and never look back.

A very special thanks goes out to my wife. She not only puts up with me but is my driving force and my toughest critic, without her none of this would be possible. She encourages me daily and is my best friend. I owe her more than I can express in writing.

Love Rich Gomez

ABOUT
AUTHOR

Richard Gomez is an author
and public speaker who helps
individuals and organizations understand how to be
a good steward by managing their money. With over a
decade of trying to break the code and reading hundreds
of books on money and finances, Richard has taken
everything he has learned it, applied it, and matched it with
the Bible. He has taught multiple church groups and
individuals giving them the tools to have a solid financial IQ
and becoming financially free.

STAY CONNECTED
FOLLOW ME

FACEBOOK
facebook.com/richardgmz

INSTAGRAM
instagram.com/richardgmz13

TIKTOK
vm.tiktok.com/ZMJm2rmsa

TWITTER
twitter.com/richardagmz

VISIT US:

SHEEPAMIDWOLVES.COM

WANT SOME BIBLICAL ENTP
MERCH?

GET UPDATES ON NEW
BOOKS

STAY CONNECTED!

CHILDREN'S
FINANCE BOOKS
COMING SOON.

SIGNUP TO OUR NEWSLETTER! VISIT:

WWW.THEBIBLICALENTREPRENEUR.COM

THE NEXT STEP
COURSE

Get the course where I guide you through the complexities?

Everything in this book is given to you in a video step-by-step video course. I will guide you and show you exactly how to do everything illustrated in this book and more.
Plus, help with setting up all your accounts from Banks to your investing accounts.
Visit:

WWW.SHEEPAMIDWOLVES.COM/COURSE

✓ Step-By-Step Video Course

✓ Over 6 Hours of Instruction

✓ Video Guide for Account Setup

✓ Lifetime Membership

✓ Completion Certificate

✓ Money Back Guarantee

For Credit Repair Kit Go to:
richcreditsolutions.com/free-video

NEED A
SPEAKER?

VISIT
RICHGMZSPEAKS.COM

Need someone to speak at your location? Featured on multiple podcasts and over the last 3 years, he has used his powerful voice to speak in schools, churches and organizations on subjects like finding purpose, overcoming the fear of failure, the power of social media, and social emotional learning in schools. He has also taught multiple classes on personal finance, investing, the power of tithing and building wealth.

Just a few years ago, Richard has been in utter debt with a dead-end job, but since then, and after reading over 200 books, Richard has broken barriers and reached new heights. His influence has been spreading quickly and we look forward to bringing it to you.

9 781647 463410